Language Lessons

Leaving Certificate English Paper 1 (Higher Level)

Martin Kieran & Frances Rocks

Gill Education
Hume Avenue
Park West
Dublin 12
www.gilleducation.ie

Gill Education is an imprint of M.H. Gill & Co.

ISBN: 978-0-7171-73242

Design and layout: Barbara Croatto

For permission to reproduce photographs, the authors and publisher gratefully acknowledge the following:
© Alamy: 17, 20, 23, 31, 37B, 39T, 39C, 42C, 126, 127, 130, 141, 145; © Ben Leto: 139; © David Levene: 62; © Getty Images: 3, 14, 28, 37T, 86B, 103, 111; © iStock: 25, 29, 33, 39B, 45, 48, 51, 53, 57, 65, 69, 83, 85, 86T, 87, 92, 96, 101, 105, 131, 136, 144; courtesy of the National Library of Ireland: 8; © The Penguin Group: 42L; © The Random House Group: 41L.

The authors and publisher have made every effort to trace all copyright holders, but if any have been inadvertently overlooked we would be pleased to make the necessary arrangement at the first opportunity.

The paper used in this book is made from the wood pulp of managed forests. For every tree felled, at least one tree is planted, thereby renewing natural resources.

CONTENTS

LEAVING CERTIFICATE PAPER 1

INTRODUCTION

'**Mature and critical literacy**' is the 'overarching educational aim of the syllabus'.

A student of English responds to a text and learns to articulate that response. Developing control and power over language is the most essential educational achievement if students are to become confident, thoughtful and discriminating adults and citizens.

Leaving Certificate English tests skills of remembering, analysing, understanding, applying, evaluating and creating.

It aims at developing the student's ability to 'adopt a variety of critical stances, to question the authority of texts and to compare and contrast texts'.

Whether you are reading a text or creating one, it's important to be aware of the following:

- Purpose
- Audience
- Register
- Content
- Style

'READING' EXAMINATION QUESTIONS

Leaving Certificate Higher level English is marked using the **PCLM** marking scheme: purpose, coherence, language and mechanics. Identifying the task is crucial both in the exam and as a life skill.

Understanding Purpose

Students need to be aware of the different types of writing that will appear in both the Comprehending and Composing sections of Paper 1 in order to pinpoint the task. Some of the main types of prose include:

- **Autobiographical writing**: describing oneself – thoughts, feelings, opinions, etc.
- **Informative writing** presents information in a logical and organised manner.
- **Narrative writing** tells a story – usually involving conflict.
- **Persuasive writing** attempts to direct the reader towards a particular viewpoint.
- **Argumentative or discursive writing** explores and discusses topics. Discursive essays are usually more balanced and impersonal.
- **Descriptive writing** places a strong emphasis on depicting things and/or people and reflecting on what has been observed.

All of these writing genres can sometimes have an aesthetic (or poetic) quality.

What am I being asked to do?

In the examination, it's essential to **study the wording** of questions very carefully before you begin writing. Highlight the key words in the question, so that you are clear about the task.

- **Outline:** Briefly describe only the main points or facts about something.
- **Comment on:** Give a critical, analytical response on subject matter and/or style of writing.
- **Explain:** Clarify by giving details and/or reasons.
- **Discuss:** Examine and distinguish the positive and negative points of something or someone.
- **Identify:** Find examples.
- **Evaluate:** Consider something carefully and decide how significant/insignificant it is.
- **Define:** Specify exactly what something means.
- **Analyse:** Consider and question closely in order to explain.
- **Illustrate:** Show by giving more information or examples to explain or prove something.
- **Compare and contrast:** Examine similarities and differences.
- **Identify parallels:** This phrase is a synonym for compare.
- **Illustrate:** Make a point and use specific examples to support it.
- **Develop your point of view:** Support the points you make through further – and more detailed – discussion, using suitable reference.

COMPREHENDING A

COMPREHENDING A

The Comprehending A questions test your ability to read, understand, analyse and respond to a particular text. This question is awarded 50 marks and has three parts.

Comprehending A parts (i) and (ii) usually deal with the content or subject matter of the text. They are sometimes referred to as 'information retrieval' questions and are each worth 15 marks.

You might be asked to summarise (in your own words) key aspects of the text. Possible questions include:

- Your observations about a character, relationship or ideas in the text.
- An outline of the writer's own views and/or lifestyle.
- Responding personally to the text.
- Your impressions of places, settings and atmospheres.
- The overall impact of the text (or particular parts of the text).

In most cases, three short paragraphs, based on three relevant, supported points, should be sufficient. Aim for 180–200 words.

Comprehending A question part (iii) usually deals with style and is worth 20 marks.

You will be asked to identify and discuss key features of the writer's language use such as:

- Does the style reinforce the writer's purpose?
- Is the language and expression appropriate to the task?
- Are the narrative and/or descriptive stylistic features effective?
- Is the writing interesting? Persuasive? Entertaining? Informative?
- How does the writer create setting and/or atmosphere?
- Are the visual images appropriate and effective?

LESSON 1: ANALYSING A WRITER'S STYLE

Learning aim: Analysing and discussing key aspects of a writer's style

Beatlebone

The following text is from Kevin Barry's novel Beatlebone *in which the author imagines the famous musician, John Lennon, making a secret visit to Ireland in 1978. In this extract, Lennon tries to book a room in a small, out-of-the-way hotel.*

BEATLEBONE

Reception is deserted but they're banging pots and pans together out the back. A demented brass band. Morning engagements only. He smells the green of bacon being fried up. Wallow in the waft of grease and smoke. Eat the pig and act the goat. He presses the bell. Nobody shows. He presses again and waits. There's no rush on. He presses again and a hatchet-faced crone appears on the tip of her witch's snout. Looks him up and down. Sour as the other Monday's milk. Double checks his ankles to see if he's got a suitcase hid down there.

Well? she says.

It's about a room, love.

She throws an eye up the clock.

This is a foxy hour to be landing into a hotel, she says.

And in denim, he says.

The reception's air is old and heavy, as in a sick room's, and the clock swings through its gloomy moments.

Do you have a reservation? she says.

I have severe ones, he says, but I do need a room.

She sucks her teeth. She opens a ledger. She raises her eyeglasses. She has a good long read of her ledger.

Does it say anything in there about a room, love?

She searches out her mouth with the tip of a green tongue.

It's about a room? he says.

With great and noble sorrow she turns and from a hook on a wooden rack takes down a key – he feels like he's been hanging from that rack for years.

The best room you can do me?

They don't differ much, she says, and switches the key for another – he'll get the worst for asking.

Payment in advance, she says.

No surprise there.

Name? she says, and he rustles one from the air.

She leads him up a stair that smells of mouse and yesteryear and they climb again to an attic floor and the eaves lean in as if they could tell a few secrets – hello? – and at the end of a dark passage they come to a scary old wooden door.

Is this where you keep the hunchback? he says.

She scowls and slides the key and turns its oily clicks.

He thanks her as he squeezes by – hello? – and for half a moment she brightens. She lays a papery hand on his – quality of mothskin; the veins ripped like junkie veins – and she whispers –

Your man? she says. You're very like him.

Not as much as I used to be, he says.

QUESTION A

i. Based on your reading of the extract, what impression do you form of John Lennon's character and personality? Support your views with reference to the text. (15)
ii. In your opinion, how does the woman's behaviour reveal her attitude towards Lennon? Support your answer with reference to the text. (15)
iii. The author's writing style has been described as lively, inventive and funny. Based on your reading of this extract, would you agree with this description? Support your answer with reference to both the content and style of the text. (20)

WRITING ABOUT CHARACTER

- Character response questions are focused firmly on **how characters reveal themselves** by what they do, say and think.
- We also learn about individuals from their **relationships** and from what others think of them.
- In analysing characters, it is important to support observations and comments with **evidence** from the text.
- In the previous extract, there are several indications about the kind of person John Lennon is. As you re-read the extract, ask yourself:

  Is he friendly or hostile?

  Does he seem relaxed or edgy?

  Is he observant?

  Does he have a sense of humour?

Sample answer for part (i)

John Lennon's character and personality is seen at the start when he has a bit of a stand-off with the woman at the reception desk. He knows she's grumpy and this proves he's a good judge of people. He is also an impatient character, pressing the bell over and over again until someone comes to reception. He is kind of polite to the 'crone' even though she is nasty enough to him at times.

Lennon is an observant sort of character who notices everything and takes in all the little details going on around him. He sees that the crone is taking her time, 'She sucks her teeth'. He notices that the top attic has a 'scary old wooden door' and he is very sarcastic to her also, in saying that the hotel is somewhere that you would keep a hunchback. There's something sad about the way he is running away and hiding himself in such a hotel. I get the impression that Lennon is a character who is full of regrets and that he has issues to work out.

Examiner's comment

- This response begins well and shows a good understanding of John Lennon's initial uneasiness in dealing with people.
- Some characteristics are mentioned, but there is a lack of follow-up commentary, e.g. 'He knows she's grumpy: "Sour as the other Monday's milk"'.
- Reference could have been made to the range of verbs ('smells', 'Wallow', 'eat', 'act', 'presses'), which show Lennon's nervous energy.
- Some expressions ('bit of', 'kind of') could also have been improved. (11/15)

Developing critical literacy to improve your answer

* Identify three distinct characteristics and organise a three-paragraph answer, using reference and/or quotation from the text.
* Describe each character trait clearly, supporting your comments with evidence. The point about Lennon's sarcastic personality could have been developed in the sample answer. What other examples of his wit or humour are apparent?
* Search for clues in the writing, e.g. Lennon does not lose his temper, but repeatedly asks for a room. What does this suggest about him?
* Work on improving expression by avoiding repetition and varying sentence length. Use alternatives for 'character', such as 'person', 'man', 'type' or 'individual'.

WRITING ABOUT STYLE

* Style is the way written (and visual) language is used to suit a specific context, purpose, or audience. **Vocabulary, syntax** (the order of words) and **sentence fluency** all contribute to the style of a piece of writing.
* The writer's **unique voice** is another essential element of style. It can be personal or formal, authoritative or reflective, objective or passionate, serious or humorous, etc.
* When reading a text, you will quickly become aware of how that particular writer uses language. A **pattern** may emerge where a certain technique is evident, e.g. in the extract from *Beatlebone*, the author breaks many of the rules of conventional punctuation. This is in keeping with the edgy, irreverent atmosphere of the scene.

In the extract from *Beatlebone*, there are other interesting aspects of the author's style. As you re-read the extract, ask yourself:

- What kind of **setting** is created?
- Is **dialogue** used effectively?
- Are there any vivid **descriptive details**?
- Is the **structure** fluent or fragmented?

Sample answer for part (iii)

The writing style of this text is very lively and unusual. It is like a short film scene where a man arrives at a run-down hotel wanting a room and doesn't get a great welcome. The writer sets the scene at the start by describing the noisy 'banging' of pots and pans in the kitchen. The visitor knows it's a strange sort of place and the reader is also drawn in to it, wondering what is going on. This very laid-back atmosphere is seen where he has to wait ages before the receptionist appears. 'There's no rush on'.

Kevin Barry creates a very unusual dramatic scene when the guest plays a cat and mouse game with the woman who takes his details. I imagine her as eccentric. The writer builds up a picture of this character as 'a hatchet-faced crone'. There is a reference to her 'green tongue' that makes her out to be even more of a witch. The image of her 'papery hand' like 'mothskin' is actually disturbing.

The inventive writing is also quite funny at times. When the receptionist asks her guest if he has a reservation, he pretends to misunderstand what she is meaning and says he has 'severe ones'. He is quite a witty character and asks her if there is a hunchback imprisoned in her attic. This use of lively humour is in contrast to the very morbid atmosphere in the old hotel. It makes the piece lively and engaging, so that the reader would like to find out what happens next in this strange hotel. Overall, this is an inventive and imaginative piece of lively writing that keeps the reader involved to find out more.

Examiner's comment

- Focuses well on style and includes some worthwhile discussion on atmosphere, characterisation and humour.
- Points are supported with suitable reference and quotation.
- Good attempt made to explain the effect of stylistic features, e.g. 'The image of her "papery hand" like "mothskin" is actually disturbing'.
- More comment on the inventive aspects of the narrative style is expected. (16/20)

Developing critical literacy to improve your answer

* It would help to focus more on the inventive features of style, referring to the surreal mood established in the opening paragraph e.g. the 'demented brass band' and 'hatchet-faced crone' suggest chaos and danger.
* A more thorough exploration of the experimental aspects of the writing would also improve the answer. The disjointed syntax ('The best room you can do me?'), snappy dialogue without regular punctuation ('Name? she says, and he rustles one from the air'), and cinematic pauses ('and the eaves lean in as if they could tell a few secrets – hello?– ') all add to the unnerving, dream-like atmosphere.
* Some of the points made have the potential for further development. There are other disturbing details: 'The reception's air is old and heavy, as in a sick room's' and 'he feels like he's been hanging from that rack for years'. Is there a sense of doom about this decaying hotel and the people in it?
* Improve expression by varying sentence length and avoiding repetition. The words 'very' and 'lively' are over-used throughout and there is some awkward language use e.g. 'misunderstand what she is meaning'.

CLASS/HOMEWORK EXERCISE

Based on the sample answer to Question A part (iii) above, write your own response to the writer's style, which has been described as lively, inventive and funny.

Allow about 15–18 minutes and aim for at least three focused, supported points. Use the comments and notes on the sample answer to help you.

Checklist: Elements of style used to engage readers

Narrative writing

- [x] First person narration, interior monologue creates empathy
- [x] Strong characterisation connects readers to the story
- [x] Dialogue discloses character and conflict
- [x] Use of tension, plot twists, absorb audience
- [x] Careful observation of setting, skilfully created mood lend credibility

Aesthetic writing

run, walk, climb, jump, talk, cry, sleep, write etc.

- [x] Descriptive details and dynamic verbs facilitate reader's involvement
- [x] Poetic techniques: personification, similes, use of repetition, rhythm enrich the reader's experience
- [x] Sound effects: alliteration, assonance onomatopoeia, increase the reader's involvement
- [x] Imagery = Auditory to hear. Visual to see. Tactile to touch, olfactory to smell and gustatory to taste.

Informative writing

- [x] Reference to historical background lends credibility
- [x] Use of data, statistics, examples add authority
- [x] Factual, accessible language increases the reader's understanding
- [x] Logical, organised structure impresses
- [x] Use of contrast and similarity aids comprehension

Personal writing

- [x] Anecdotal, personal approach creates empathy
- [x] Rhetorical devices: repetition, rhetorical questions, inclusive/superlative language reinforce the message ('we', 'our'; happiest, highest, fastest)
- [x] Emphatic, emotional verbs affect reader (really)
- [x] Humour lightens the message, strengthens the bond between writer and reader
- [x] Sense of audience inspires reader's sympathy

LESSON 2: WRITING ABOUT CHARACTERS

Learning aim: To create a successful character study based on a text

Images of Constance Markievicz

In this radio talk text, Ivy Bannister remembers Countess Constance Markievicz (1868–1927), one of Ireland's best-known revolutionary figures.

In 1914 at the age of forty-six the Countess Markievicz posed as Joan of Arc[1] to raise funds for the Irish Women's Franchise League. She stands, dramatic in her armour, sword uplifted, eyes glowing with divine fervour. It's a witty photograph that reveals, I believe, how clearly Countess Markievicz identified with her sainted predecessor, another selfless, cheery nationalist bent upon sending the English packing.

The image must have horrified Constance's mother, Lady Gore-Booth of Sligo, who didn't want a rebel heroine for a daughter. For in earlier years, when Lady Gore-Booth could shape her daughter's image, Constance was always pictured in the conventional, ascendancy[2] way. At twelve, she was painted as the well-dressed daughter of the big house, her back aristocratically straight, as she keeps watch over her younger sister.

By eighteen, she was photographed as a debutante, exquisitely formal in snowy white, gloves to the elbow, a fan and dainty satin pumps. Through presenting her thus at Dublin Castle and in Queen Victoria's court, Lady Gore-Booth intended her daughter to find her destiny in marriage to another moneyed member of the Protestant ascendancy, and in half-a-dozen healthy offspring to perpetuate[3] her class.

Young Constance had different ideas. Liking nothing better than a wild gallop across the countryside, she remained unimpressed by her swarms of suitors.[4]

'Jam, jelly and bread,' she snorted into her diary about one. She made another toss his hat into the air for her to shoot at. And when a third slipped his hand onto her thigh at a formal dinner, she lifted it gleefully into the air, announcing, 'Just look at what I've found in my lap'.

Fortunately, Constance was blessed with an artistic ability that enabled her to break from expectation. It began as a few lessons during the season. Then after persistent badgering, she was allowed study art full time at the Slade[5] in London.

Now with Lady Gore-Booth safely distant in Sligo, the young woman began to forge her own image. She had herself photographed – smocked and smoking – in her studio, a dishevelled Bohemian chaos. Her mother turned a blind eye, hoping perhaps that the phase would pass, and that time might see her daughter return to the stately fold.

1. 15th-century French martyr
2. Privileged class
3. Continue
4. Would-be marriage partners
5. Renowned art college

Instead, the industrious art student was accepted by the Atelier Julian[6] in Paris, where she bought herself a ring and declared herself married to art. Now, at the ripe age of thirty, Constance did fall in love, totally inappropriately with a penniless Polish Count, another art student, who, although six years her junior, had already been married, and was a father and a Catholic to boot.

Blithely, Constance commemorated the event with a photograph, upon which her mother must have gazed with horrified fascination. For in the photograph, Count Casimir's arm is draped informally around Constance's waist and they are both dressed in bicycling gear. It was a daring, even shocking pose for 1899 for Constance's knickerbockers reveal her legs completely beneath the knee.

To my mind, this splendid, happy photograph marks a point of no return, shattering forever her mother's picture of Constance, declaring in black and white that whatever Constance soon-to-be Markievicz might choose to do with her future, it would be both whole-hearted and unpredictable.

6. Prestigious art studio

QUESTION A

Outline, in your own words, three of Constance Markievicz's distinctive character traits. Support your answer with reference to the written text. (15)

Sample answer

Having read the above extract, I think that Constance is a very intelligent and very advanced modern-thinking character. She seems to be very much ahead of her time. As an attractive debutante, she was confident enough to make her own choices in life – particularly in her dealings with her 'swarms' of suitors. I get the impression that she treated some of them like irritating insects.

It's clear from the passage that Countess Markievicz knew her own mind and was determined to fulfil her own ambitions. Her 'persistent badgering' tells me that she had a very strong personality that enabled her to break away from family expectations and complete her art studies in London.

Markievicz was obviously romantic and idealistic. Her lifestyle was unconventional and she was happy to 'fall in love, totally inappropriately' with someone who would not have been the choice of her domineering mother. For me, the words 'whole-hearted and unpredictable' are a perfect description of this exceptional woman.

Examiner's comment

- Despite the awkward opening (over-use of 'very'), this is a well-focused character study and a successful response overall.
- Points are clearly stated and well-organised into paragraphs.
- Effective use is made of reference and quotation throughout.
- Generally, expression is controlled, varied and fluent ('As an attractive debutante... of suitors'). (13/15)

CLASS/HOMEWORK EXERCISE

QUESTION A

(ii) From your reading of this extract, what impression do you form of Lady Gore-Booth? Support your view with reference to the text. (15)

Allow about 12–14 minutes and aim for three focused, supported points in short paragraphs.

Prompt!

- Is Lady Gore-Booth class-conscious?
- What part does social status play in her expectations?
- Is she tolerant or narrow-minded?
- Does she encourage her spirited daughter?
- Is she a woman who is typical of her time?

LESSON 3: DISCUSSING NARRATIVE STYLE

Learning aim: To analyse and discuss key aspects of narrative style

The Great Gatsby

The opening section of Scott Fitzgerald's The Great Gatsby *introduces the narrator, Nick Carraway, and establishes the novel's setting. The story begins in 1922 when Nick rents a small house in West Egg, an area on Long Island, New York. The mansion next door belongs to the mysterious millionaire, Jay Gatsby. Across the bay in East Egg live Nick's cousin, Daisy, and her husband, Tom Buchanan.*

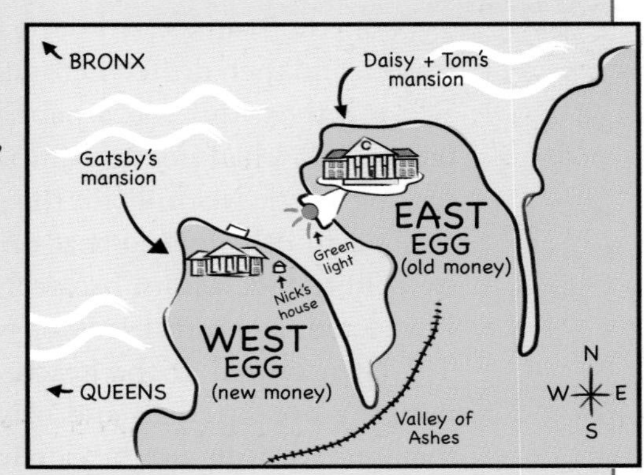

Read the following extract carefully, paying particular attention to the writer's style.

THE GREAT GATSBY

It was a matter of chance that I should have rented a house in one of the strangest communities in North America. It was on that slender riotous island which extends itself due east of New York – and where there are, among other natural curiosities, two unusual formations of land. Twenty miles from the city a pair of enormous eggs, identical in contour and separated only by a courtesy bay, jut out into the most domesticated body of salt water in the Western hemisphere, the great wet barnyard of Long Island Sound. They are not perfect ovals – like the egg in the Columbus story, they are both crushed flat at the contact end – but their physical resemblance must be a source of perpetual confusion to the gulls that fly overhead. To the wingless a more interesting phenomenon is their dissimilarity in every particular except shape and size.

I lived at West Egg, the – well, the less fashionable of the two, though this is a most superficial tag to express the bizarre and not a little sinister contrast between them. My house was at the very tip of the egg, only fifty yards from the Sound, and squeezed between two huge places that rented for twelve or fifteen thousand a season. The one on my right was a colossal affair by any standard – it was a factual imitation of some Hotel de Ville in Normandy, with a tower on one side, spanking new under a thin beard of raw ivy, and a marble swimming pool, and more than forty acres of lawn and garden. It was Gatsby's mansion. Or, rather, as I didn't know Mr. Gatsby, it was a mansion inhabited by a gentleman of that name. My own house was an eyesore, but it was a small eyesore, and it had been overlooked, so I had a view of the water, a partial view of my neighbour's lawn, and the consoling proximity of millionaires – all for eighty dollars a month.

Across the courtesy bay the white palaces of fashionable East Egg glittered along the water, and the history of the summer really begins on the evening I drove over there to have dinner with the Tom Buchanans. Daisy was my second cousin once removed, and I'd known Tom in college. And just after the war I spent two days with them in Chicago.

Her husband, among various physical accomplishments, had been one of the most powerful ends that ever played football at New Haven – a national figure in a way, one of those men who reach such an acute limited excellence at twenty-one that everything afterward savours of anti-climax. His family were enormously wealthy – even in college his freedom with money was a matter for reproach – but now he'd left Chicago and come east in a fashion that rather took your breath away: for instance he'd brought down a string of polo ponies from Lake Forest. It was hard to realize that a man in my own generation was wealthy enough to do that.

Why they came east I don't know. They had spent a year in France, for no particular reason, and then drifted here and there unrestfully wherever people played polo and were rich together. This was a permanent move, said Daisy over the telephone, but I didn't believe it – I had no sight into Daisy's heart but I felt that Tom would drift on forever seeking a little wistfully for the dramatic turbulence of some irrecoverable football game.

And so it happened that on a warm windy evening I drove over to East Egg to see two old friends whom I scarcely knew at all. Their house was even more elaborate than I expected, a cheerful red-and-white Georgian Colonial mansion, overlooking the bay. The lawn started at the beach and ran toward the front door for a quarter of a mile, jumping over sundials and brick walks and burning gardens – finally when it reached the house drifting up the side in bright vines as though from the momentum of its run. The front was broken by a line of French windows, glowing now with reflected gold and wide open to the warm windy afternoon, and Tom Buchanan in riding clothes was standing with his legs apart on the front porch.

He had changed since his New Haven years. Now he was a sturdy straw-haired man of thirty with a rather hard mouth and a supercilious manner. Two shining arrogant eyes had established dominance over his face and gave him the appearance of always leaning aggressively forward. Not even the effeminate swank of his riding clothes could hide the enormous power of that body – he seemed to fill those glistening boots until he strained the top lacing, and you could see a great pack of muscle shifting when his shoulder moved under his thin coat. It was a body capable of enormous leverage – a cruel body.

Some stylistic features

◆ **Narrative voice** ◆ **Tone** ◆ **Detailed description** ◆ **Imagery and symbolism**

- Consider the effectiveness of Fitzgerald's use of **narrative voice**. Nick Carraway is both the storyteller and a participant in the action. Does this make him a reliable narrator?
- The **tone** varies from reflective commentary to criticism and satire. Nick shows readers his attitude to 'one of the strangest communities in North America'.
- Numerous examples of **detailed description** (of places and people) throughout the extract add realism.
- Effective **imagery and symbolism** highlight revealing aspects of the 'world' Fitzgerald has created.

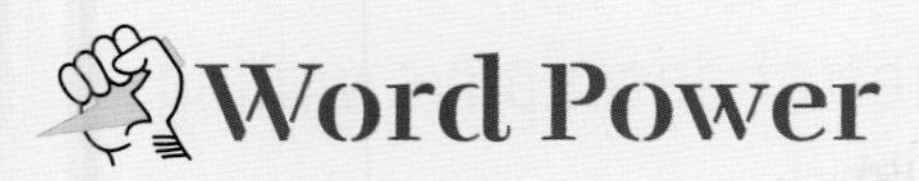

Close analysis of Fitzgerald's language provides an understanding of the extract and is essential for answering questions successfully. The following discussion notes focus on key words and phrases that illustrate the writer's distinctive style.

* Gatsby's mansion is located in 'the less fashionable' West Egg. Although it is lavish, it is vulgar and unsophisticated. Nick **sneers** at it for being unattractive and looking like a copy of a distinguished French villa, 'some Hôtel de Ville in Normandy'. This suggests its design is inappropriately grandiose. It is also significant that it is an imitation. Does this imply that the mansion's owner is equally shallow and pretentious?
* Fitzgerald's use of **personification** in the phrase 'a thin beard of raw ivy' is effective in again demanding comparison with its owner. The image is almost comic, but might indicate innocence and vulnerability, as well as a wish for privacy.
* Nick's rented house is also in West Egg. He mocks it as a 'small eyesore' and describes it as being 'squeezed between two huge places'. This suggests inequality and oppression. Is Fitzgerald simply **criticising the class system**?
* Daisy and Tom live on the other side of the bay. While that area is expensive and luxurious, it seems to have a kind of **fairytale** beauty: 'the white palaces of fashionable East Egg glittered along the water'. The word 'palaces' evokes connotations of aristocracy while 'glittered' perhaps suggests magic and even falseness. While he is clearly fascinated with East Egg, Nick's caustic comments suggest that he finds little enough comfort in 'the consoling proximity of millionaires'.
* The 'more elaborate' Buchanans' house is built in 'Georgian colonial' style and gives the impression of illustrious **tradition**. Fitzgerald's use of plurals suggests that the family is excessively well-to-do. The expansive lawn leads on to 'sundials and brick walks and burning gardens'. Nick is enchanted by his first glimpse of the rich interior, 'glowing now with reflected gold'.
* The first image of Tom Buchanan is one of power and domination. Nick notices Tom's 'hard mouth' and his 'shining arrogant eyes'. Does he see Tom as a symbol of privilege? Is there also a suggestion of brutality about Buchanan? For the most part, Tom is portrayed as an unpleasant, **intimidating** figure who still retains the powerful physique of the star football player – 'a cruel body'.

CLASS/HOMEWORK EXERCISE

QUESTION A

(iii) Based on what you have read in the extract from *The Great Gatsby*, do you agree that Scott Fitzgerald is both a skilful writer and a perceptive observer of human nature? Support your answer with reference to the text. (20)

Allow about 15–18 minutes and aim for at least three focused points. The notes above will be helpful in responding to the question on the writer's style.

LESSON 4: ANALYSING DESCRIPTIVE WRITING

Learning aim: To analyse and discuss key features of descriptive writing

The Grapes of Wrath

This text by the American writer, John Steinbeck, is taken from The Grapes of Wrath. *Set during the 1930s Great Depression, the novel tells the story of a family displaced from their Oklahoma farm following the devastating Dust Bowl storms that wreck their crops.*

Read the following extract carefully, paying particular attention to the writer's descriptive language.

The Grapes of Wrath

The wind grew stronger. The rain crust broke and the dust lifted up out of the fields and drove gray plumes[1] into the air like sluggish smoke. The corn threshed the wind and made a dry, rushing sound. The finest dust did not settle back to earth now, but disappeared into the darkening sky.

The wind grew stronger, whisked under stones, carried up straws and old leaves, and even little clods, marking its course as it sailed across the fields. The air and the sky darkened and through them the sun shone redly, and there was a raw sting in the air. During a night the wind raced faster over the land, dug cunningly among the rootlets[2] of the corn, and the corn fought the wind with its weakened leaves until the roots were freed by the prying wind and then each stalk settled wearily sideways toward the earth and pointed the direction of the wind.

The dawn came, but no day. In the gray sky a red sun appeared, a dim red circle that gave a little light, like dusk; and as that day advanced, the dusk slipped back toward darkness, and the wind cried and whimpered over the fallen corn.

Men and women huddled in their houses, and they tied handkerchiefs over their noses when they went out, and wore goggles to protect their eyes.

When the night came again it was black night, for the stars could not pierce the dust to get down, and the window lights could not even spread beyond their own yards. Now the dust was evenly mixed with the air, and emulsion of dust and air. Houses were shut tight, and cloth wedged around doors and windows, but the dust came in so thinly that it could not be seen in the air, and it settled like pollen on the chairs and tables, on the dishes. The people brushed it from their shoulders. Little lines of dust lay at the door sills.[3]

In the middle of that night the wind passed on and left the land quiet. The dust-filled air muffled sound more completely than fog does. The people, lying in their beds, heard the wind stop. They awakened when the rushing wind was gone.

1. Grey column of smoke
2. Small roots
3. Doorsteps

They lay quietly and listened deep into the stillness. Then the roosters crowed, and their voices were muffled, and the people stirred restlessly in their beds and wanted the morning. They knew it would take a long time for the dust to settle out of the air. In the morning the dust hung like fog, and the sun was as red as ripe new blood. All day the dust sifted down from the sky, and the next day it sifted down. An even blanket covered the earth. It settled on the corn, piled up on the tops of the fence posts, piled up on the wires; it settled on roofs, blanketed the weeds and trees.

The people came out of their houses and smelled the hot stinging air and covered their noses from it. And the children came out of the houses, but they did not run or shout as they would have done after a rain. Men stood by their fences and looked at the ruined corn, drying fast now, only a little green showing through the film of dust. The men were silent and they did not move often. And the women came out of the houses to stand beside their men – to feel whether this time the men would break.[4] The women studied the men's faces secretly, for the corn could go, as long as something else remained. The children stood nearby drawing figures in the dust with bare toes, and the children sent exploring senses out to see whether men and women would break.

The children peeked at the faces of the men and women, and then drew careful lines in the dust with their toes. Horses came to the watering troughs and nuzzled the water to clear the surface dust. After a while the faces of the watching men lost their bemused perplexity and became hard and angry and resistant. Then the women knew that they were safe and that there was no break. Then they asked, What'll we do? And the men replied, I don't know. But, it was all right. The women knew it was all right, and the watching children knew it was all right. Women and children knew deep in themselves that no misfortune was too great to bear if their men were whole. The women went into the houses to their work, and the children began to play, but cautiously at first. As the day went forward the sun became less red. It flared down on the dust-blanketed land. The men sat in the doorways of their houses; their hands were busy with sticks and little rocks. The men sat still – thinking – figuring.[5]

4. Give up hope
5. Looking for a solution

Some stylistic features

- **Detailed description** • **Forceful verbs** • **Imagery** • **Personification**
- **Repetition** • **Atmosphere**

Word Power

Close analysis of John Steinbeck's language provides an understanding of the extract and is essential for answering questions successfully. The following discussion notes focus on key words and phrases that illustrate the writer's descriptive skill.

The extract begins with a bleak depiction of the Dust Bowl. **Forceful verbs** ('broke, 'threshed') reflect the power and violence of nature. Steinbeck suggests the slow spread of unease as 'corn fought the wind'. The destructive force of the Dust Bowl is depicted as a backward life cycle, a regression from fertile green to a dead and dusty brown.

Painstaking detail gives us a picture of the extraordinary scene. Dust overwhelms Oklahoma, clouding the air and even blocking out the sun. Families hide indoors, covering their noses with handkerchiefs and wearing 'goggles to protect their eyes'.

The hostility of the environment is evoked through vivid **colour imagery and harsh sounding metaphors** to describe the setting. The ominous sun is 'red as ripe new blood'. Other jarring sound effects ('raw sting', 'hot stinging air') emphasise people's pain and suffering. The repeated references to red and gray are dramatic, highlighting the surreal atmosphere.

The author imagines the relentless wind 'as it sailed across the fields'.

The unstoppable dust is presented as a living entity, something that has consciously intruded on the lives of people as they cower in their beds. It 'came in so thinly' like a thief in the night. Such **personification** is a powerful literary device to suggest the devastating power of nature.

Farm women and children wonder if the severe drought and the crop failures will cause their men's spirits and wills to break. Through a blurred, brooding mood, Steinbeck conveys the helplessness and growing anger of these impoverished farmers. Is he **foreshadowing** further conflict and tragedy ahead?

CLASS/HOMEWORK EXERCISE

QUESTION A

(iii) Based on what you have read in the above extract from *The Grapes of Wrath*, do you agree that John Steinbeck's descriptive writing is rich in language and imagery? (20)

Allow about 15–18 minutes and aim for at least three focused, supported points. The notes above on descriptive writing will be helpful in responding to the question.

LESSON 5: PERSONAL RESPONSES

Learning aim: To write an effective personal response to a text

How *Groundhog Day* Saved My Life

In this short personal opinion piece, Paul Hannam describes the impact of a popular Hollywood movie.

GROUNDHOG DAY

1. Can a movie change your life? How about a comedy? How about *Groundhog Day*? I believe that this wonderful film contains remarkable wisdom that can help you be happier and more fulfilled. There are three transformative principles at its heart that I have used to improve my life and that you can use to improve yours, too.

2. Principle number one: practice makes perfect. *Groundhog Day* is a sustained, ingenious experiment in how to make the most of every day and live your life to the full. Bill Murray's character, Phil Connors, learns how to be incredibly resourceful as he turns a miserable day into a great day through consistent practice – until he masters the art of living his one day to the full. I try to improve every day, too, experimenting with new ways of thinking, feeling and behaving so that I can remain spontaneous, agile and open to change.

3. Ask yourself: 'What could I think, say and do differently today?' Then instead of living on autopilot, replaying the same old patterns, you can create a new and better experience whenever you want.

4. The second principle: improve the quality of your inner life. *Groundhog Day* is a story of self-awareness, self-improvement and ultimately self-transformation. Phil does not transform his character through attaining more power, wealth or status. He cannot change his place or time, so he has to change himself. He simplifies his life to the essence, to what is most significant – like being aware and caring for others.

5. This has been a big lesson for me. It took me many years to realise that most of the goals we strive for, such as financial success, travel and popularity, count for far less than we expect. Now I focus on getting my inner life right first, on feeling a sense of wellbeing irrespective of what is happening in my outer life. When you do the same, you will be calmer and happier.

6. The third principle: appreciate that you have everything you need to be happy now. *Groundhog Day* is the tale of how Phil gradually discovers that what he thought was hell turns out to be heaven. He learns to love the same town, people and activities that he had previously hated. Nothing alters except his attitude. I used to be restless all the time, moving house every year or so, distracting myself with new businesses and even emigrating to California. Now I focus on appreciating what I have in the knowledge that I need nothing more to feel happy now.

7. So every time you feel low or suffer a setback, ask yourself: 'What is good about my life now?' and, even better, write down the answers in a journal. The more you focus on being grateful and appreciative, the happier you will be. If you want to get out of a rut, try changing yourself before looking to change your circumstances.

8. I regard *Groundhog Day* as a masterclass in how to live. Trapped in time, Phil can and indeed does try every possible way to live until he discovers the ideal one based on creativity, compassion and contribution. He learns one of the greatest lessons in life. We create our own reality. We have the choice to make today and every day either sad or happy, dull or inspiring, meaningless or fulfilling. You can bring whatever mindset you choose to the next 24 hours.

9. This is an extraordinary gift that we often overlook, and there is no better example of its priceless value than *Groundhog Day*. You can make today better than yesterday; you can improve your life one day at a time.

Some stylistic features

◆ **Sense of intimacy** ◆ **Variety of tones** ◆ **Simple language** ◆ **Rhetorical techniques** ◆ **Anecdotes**

Word Power

Close analysis of Paul Hannam's language provides a greater understanding of the extract. The following discussion notes focus on key stylistic techniques used by the writer to convey his views.

The article aims for a sense of intimacy and **shared experience** between the writer and the reader ('When you do the same, you will be calmer and happier').

The opening paragraph provides a **succinct** introduction and invites the reader to engage with the article.

A **logical** approach is applied to give weight to his argument, for example the three transformative principles are broken down and explained.).

A **variety of interesting tones** is used throughout to appeal to the audience: – personal ('I believe'); reflective ('This has been a big lesson for me'); moralistic ('We create our own reality'); persuasive ('I regard *Groundhog Day* as a masterclass in how to live'); didactic ('The more you focus on being grateful and appreciative, the happier you will be').

The language is simple and engaging, appropriate to the clear, coherent, **focused** points.

Effective **rhetorical techniques**, particularly questions and repetition, add emphasis throughout ('Can a movie change your life?'). The article also relies heavily on inclusive personal pronouns ('I', 'you', 'we').

Other features include the use of anecdotes (Paragraph 6), emotional appeal (Paragraph 7) and varied sentence length (Paragraph 8).

QUESTION A

Paul Hannam asserts that the movie *Groundhog Day* can make people 'happier and more fulfilled'. Give your personal response to Hannam's claim, supporting your answer with reference to the text. (15)

Sample answer

Paul Hannam is obviously a fan of Groundhog Day and appears to live his life by it. The film's central character 'has to change himself' and this is what makes all the difference. I don't doubt that the writer's own life has been greatly affected by the movie, but I'm not sure the same impact will be felt by everyone else who sees it.

Hannam recommends 'consistent practice' to eventually ensure that a person will learn to live every day to the full. Again, this strikes me as being slightly airy-fairy. Real life is often filled with pressures that mean most of us simply can't always feel good – even though we would like to. What exactly does Hannan mean by creating 'a new and better experience'? This is too vague to mean anything. Surely, if it was so easy, doctors would be out of work and patients would be watching Bill Murray instead.

It's not that I want to be cynical, but I found the article general and unrealistic. Even though Hannam seems sincere about being positive, there was just too much hippy 'mindset' jargon and wishful thinking for my liking.

Examiner's comment

- A well-focused personal response that addresses the question directly and challenges the writer's views effectively ('I'm not sure the same impact will be felt by everyone else who sees it').
- Clear points about the vague, general arguments within the text are impressive ('this strikes me as being slightly airy-fairy').
- Expression is varied, controlled and succinct ('It's not that I want to be cynical, but I found the article general and unrealistic').
- Key points are aptly supported with suitable quotations.
- A confident, successful response. (15/15)

CLASS/HOMEWORK EXERCISE

QUESTION A

(ii) Based on what you have read in the extract by Paul Hannan, to what extent do you agree that the article is both engaging and inspiring? Support your answer with reference to both the content and style of the text. (20)

Allow about 15–18 minutes and aim for at least three focused, supported points in short paragraphs. Use the comments and notes on the sample answer to help you.

LESSON 6: ANALYSING ATTITUDES

Comprehending A

Learning aim: To analyse attitudes and relationships within a text

To Kill a Mockingbird

Harper Lee's classic American novel, To Kill a Mockingbird, *tells the story of Scout (the narrator) and her brother, Jem – children growing up in Maycomb, Alabama during the 1930s. Along with their friend, Dill, the children become entranced with the idea of getting a glimpse of their reclusive and unseen neighbours, the Radleys.*

Read the following extract carefully, paying particular attention to how the Radley family is portrayed.

To Kill a Mockingbird

The Radley Place fascinated Dill. In spite of our warnings and explanations it drew him as the moon draws water, but drew him no nearer than the light-pole on the corner, a safe distance from the Radley gate. There he would stand, his arm around the fat pole, staring and wondering.

The Radley Place jutted into a sharp curve beyond our house. Walking south, one faced its porch; the sidewalk turned and ran beside the lot.[1] The house was low, was once white with a deep front porch and green shutters, but had long ago darkened to the colour of the slate-grey yard around it. Rain-rotten shingles drooped over the eaves of the verandah; oak trees kept the sun away. The remains of a picket[2] drunkenly guarded the front yard – a 'swept' yard that was never swept – where johnson grass and rabbit-tobacco[3] grew in abundance.

Inside the house lived a malevolent phantom.[4] People said he existed, but Jem and I had never seen him. People said he went out at night when the moon was high, and peeped in windows. When people's azaleas froze in a cold snap, it was because he had breathed on them. Any stealthy small crimes committed in Maycomb were his work. Once the town was terrorized by a series of morbid nocturnal[5] events: people's chickens and household pets were found mutilated; although the culprit was Crazy Addie, who eventually drowned himself in Barker's Eddy, people still looked at the Radley Place, unwilling to discard their initial suspicions. A Negro would not pass the Radley Place at night, he would cut across to the sidewalk opposite and whistle as he walked. The Maycomb school grounds adjoined the back of the Radley lot; from the Radley chicken-yard tall pecan trees shook their fruit into the school yard, but the nuts lay untouched by the children: Radley pecans would kill you. A baseball hit into the Radley yard was a lost ball and no questions asked.

---

1. Site
2. Wooden fence
3. Weeds
4. Evil spirit
5. Nightly

The misery of that house began many years before Jem and I were born. The Radleys, welcome anywhere in town, kept to themselves, a predilection[6] unforgivable in Maycomb. They did not go to church, Maycomb's principal recreation, but worshipped at home; Mrs Radley seldom if ever crossed the street for a mid-morning coffee break with her neighbours, and certainly never joined a missionary circle. Mr Radley walked to town at eleven-thirty every morning and came back promptly at twelve, sometimes carrying a brown paper bag that the neighbourhood assumed contained the family groceries. I never knew how old Mr Radley made his living – Jem said he 'bought cotton', a polite term for doing nothing – but Mr Radley and his wife had lived there with their two sons as long as anybody could remember.

The shutters and doors of the Radley house were closed on Sundays, another thing alien to Maycomb's ways: closed doors meant illness and cold weather only. Of all days Sunday was the day for formal afternoon visiting: ladies wore corsets, men wore coats, children wore shoes. But to climb the Radley front steps and call, 'He-y', of a Sunday afternoon was something their neighbours never did.

6. Way of behaving

QUESTION A

(i) What evidence does the writer offer to show that the Radley family was looked upon with suspicion by their neighbours? (15)

Sample answer

Based on the description given by the narrator, everyone in the neighbourhood believes that the Radley home is not a welcoming place and to stay away at all costs. The 'darkened' house is described as being 'low' and out of sight, suggesting that the family has something to hide. Over the years, myths have grown about 'a malevolent phantom' occupying the house and terrifying children. The narrator mentions the 'misery' of the place.

Dill and the others are 'fascinated' by the Radleys who very obviously neglect their home. The outside yard is overgrown with weeds and was 'never swept', perhaps indicating that they are irresponsible and even dangerous. The fact that the family is associated with evil and immediately blamed for any local crime is further evidence that they are constantly under suspicion and treated with prejudice.

Almost everything the Radleys do is 'alien to Maycomb's ways'. They keep to themselves and refuse to join in local community activities. Even on Sundays when most people are at church, their doors 'were closed'. Such anti-social behaviour makes them outsiders in Maycomb – yet another reason why the Radleys are so distrusted.

Examiner's comment

- A very successful response that addresses the core question directly, i.e. finding evidence of the neighbours' suspicions towards the Radley family.
- Succinct points are well-organised into paragraphs and very good use is made of reference and quotation.
- Controlled expression integrating quotes into critical comments adds fluency.
- Rounded off effectively using 'distrusted' as an alternate to 'suspected'. (15/15)

CLASS/HOMEWORK EXERCISE

QUESTION A

(ii) What does the extract reveal about the local Maycomb community and their attitudes? (15)

Allow about 12–14 minutes and aim for three focused, supported points in short paragraphs. Use the comments and notes on the sample answer to help you.

Prompt!

- Is Maycomb a friendly community?
- What part do gossip and rumours play in town life?
- Do local people know one another's business?
- Are there any signs of racial divisions?
- Is religion important to the community?

LESSON 7: SELECTING EVIDENCE

Learning aim: To select relevant evidence from a text

The Road to Wigan Pier

The passage below is taken from The Road to Wigan Pier, *written by George Orwell in 1937 after he visited the industrial north of England.*

THE ROAD TO WIGAN PIER

SHEFFIELD, I SUPPOSE, could justly claim to be called the ugliest town in the Old World: its inhabitants, who want it to be pre-eminent[1] in everything, very likely do make that claim for it. It has a population of half a million and it contains fewer decent buildings than the average East Anglian village of five hundred. And the stench! If at rare moments you stop smelling sulphur it is because you have begun smelling gas. Even the shallow river that runs through the town is usually bright yellow with some chemical or other.

Once I halted in the street and counted the factory chimneys I could see; there were thirty-three of them, but there would have been far more if the air had not been obscured by smoke. One scene especially lingers in my mind. A frightful patch of waste ground (somehow, up there, a patch of waste ground attains a squalor that would be impossible even in London) trampled bare of grass and littered with newspapers and old saucepans.

To the right an isolated row of gaunt[2] four-roomed houses, dark red, blackened by smoke. To the left an interminable vista of factory chimneys, chimney beyond chimney, fading away into a dim blackish haze. Behind me a railway embankment made of the slag[3] from furnaces. In front, across the patch of waste ground, a cubical building of red and yellow brick, with the sign 'Thomas Grocock, Haulage Contractor'.

At night, when you cannot see the hideous shapes of the houses and the blackness of everything, a town like Sheffield assumes a kind of sinister magnificence. Sometimes the drifts of smoke are rosy with sulphur, and serrated[4] flames, like circular saws, squeeze themselves out from beneath the cowls[5] of the foundry chimneys. Through the open doors of foundries you see fiery serpents of iron being hauled to and fro by redlit boys,[6] and you hear the whizz and thump of steam hammers and the scream of the iron under the blow.

1. Outstanding
2. Ghostly
3. Waste
4. Jagged
5. Covers
6. Furnace apprentices

The pottery towns are almost equally ugly in a pettier way. Right in among the rows of tiny blackened houses, part of the street as it were, are the 'pot banks' – conical brick chimneys like gigantic burgundy bottles buried in the soil and belching their smoke almost in your face. You come upon monstrous clay chasms hundreds of feet across and almost as deep, with little rusty tubs creeping on chain railways up one side, and on the other workmen clinging like samphire-gatherers[7] and cutting into the face of the cliff with their picks. I passed that way in snowy weather, and even the snow was black. The best thing one can say for the pottery towns is that they are fairly small and stop abruptly. Less than ten miles away you can stand in undefiled country, on the almost naked hills, and the pottery towns are only a smudge in the distance.

When you contemplate such ugliness as this, there are two questions that strike you. First, is it inevitable? Secondly, does it matter?

7. Shoreline plant pickers

Word Power

Close analysis of Orwell's language provides an understanding of the extract and is essential for answering questions successfully. The following discussion notes focus on key words and phrases that illustrate the writer's descriptive skills.

Orwell regards Sheffield as a hideous, frightful, ugly, foul-smelling town ruined by industrial pollution. **Vivid details** ('you have begun smelling gas', 'thirty-three' chimneys, 'old saucepans') graphically convey the repulsive reality.

He writes from **personal** experience ('Behind me a railway embankment') and is brutally direct about his dislike of the place and its inhabitants, whom he considers arrogant.

Repetition ('blackish', 'blackened', 'black'; 'ugliest', 'ugly', 'ugliness') adds emphasis and enhances our sense of the unhealthy, oppressive atmosphere.

Gothic language ('gaunt four-roomed houses', 'hideous shapes', 'sinister magnificence') suggests gloom and fear throughout.

Vivid **colour imagery** ('bright yellow' river, 'houses, dark red', 'gigantic burgundy bottles') has a dramatic effect.

Personification adds immediacy, bringing the town to life – 'scream of the iron', naked hills'.

CLASS/HOMEWORK EXERCISE

QUESTION A

(i) Orwell claims that Sheffield is England's 'ugliest town'. In your opinion, which three pieces of evidence most effectively support his claim? In each case, briefly explain your choice. (15)

Allow about 12–14 minutes and aim for three focused, supported points in short paragraphs. The notes above on descriptive writing will be helpful in responding to this question.

LESSON 8: IDENTIFYING CHARACTER TRAITS

Learning aim: To read a written text closely and identify particular character traits

Solar

Ian McEwan's novel, Solar, focuses on climate change. In this extract, the central character, Michael Beard, is travelling by train to a conference where he is to make a speech about climate change. Sitting opposite a stranger on the train, Beard is considering whether to eat a bag of crisps.

SOLAR

Right before him on the table, shimmering through his barely parted lashes, were the salt and vinegar crisps, and just beyond the packet was a plastic bottle of mineral water belonging to the young man. Beard wondered whether he should be looking over the notes for his speech, but general travel fatigue as well as the lunchtime drinks had rendered him, for the moment, inert, and he believed he knew the material well enough, and on a card in his top pocket were various useful quotes.

As for the snack, he wanted it less than he did, but he still wanted it. Certain of those industrial compounds might stir his metabolism into wakefulness. It was his palate, rather than his stomach, that was looking forward to the acidic tang of the dust coating each brittle slice. He had shown decent restraint – the train had been moving for several minutes now – and there was no good reason to hold back.

He pulled himself up in his seat and leaned forward, elbows on the table, hands propping his chin for several reflective seconds, gaze fixed on the gaudy wrapper, silver, red and blue, with cartoon animals cavorting below a Union Jack. So childish of him, this infatuation, so weak, so harmful, a microcosm of all past errors and folly, of that impatient way he had of having to have what he wanted instantly.

He took the bag in both hands and pulled its neck apart, discharging a clammy fragrance of frying fat and vinegar. It was an artful laboratory simulation of the corner fish and chip shop, an enactment of fond memories and desire and nationhood. That flag was a considered choice. He lifted clear a single crisp between forefinger and thumb, replaced the bag on the table, and sat back. He was a man to take his pleasures seriously. The trick was to set the fragment on the centre of the tongue and, after a moment's spreading sensation, push the potato up hard to shatter against the roof of the mouth. His theory was that the rigid irregular surface caused tiny abrasions in the soft flesh into which salt and chemicals poured, creating a mild and distinctive pleasure-pain.

Like a master of wine at a grand tasting, he had closed his eyes. When he opened them he was staring into the level grey-blue gaze of the man opposite. Feeling only slightly ashamed, Beard made a gesture of impatience and looked away.

He knew how he must have appeared, a plump fool of a certain age communing intensely with a morsel of junk food. He had been behaving as though alone. So what? As long as he harmed or offended no one, that was his right. He no longer cared much what others thought of him. There were few benefits in growing older, and this was one. In a simple assertion of selfhood, rather than to satisfy his contemptible needs, he put out a hand to take another crisp, and as he did so, met again the other man's stare.

It was narrow, hard, unblinking, expressive of little beyond a ferocious curiosity. It occurred to Beard that he might be sitting across from a psychopath. So be it. He could be a bit of one himself. The salty residue from the first round gave him the impression that he was bleeding from the gums. He slumped back in his seat, opened his mouth and repeated the experience, although this time he kept his eyes open. Inevitably, the second crisp was less piquant, less surprising, less penetrating than the first, and it was precisely this shortfall, this sensual disappointment, that prompted the need, familiar to drug addicts, to increase the dose. He would eat two crisps at once.

QUESTION A

(i) Outline, in your own words, three of Michael Beard's distinctive character traits. Support your answer with reference to the written text. (15)

Sample answer

Michael Beard strikes me as a natural worrier. Obsessive. A man who turns everything into a drama. Something as simple as eating a few crisps is suddenly life-changing. A major crisis. Never at ease, he frets over his speech and 'wondered whether he should be looking over the notes'. An indecisive character.

Beard is also a born observer. He notices even the smallest details around him. The bag of crisps is singled out for special attention, with its 'gaudy wrapper, silver, red and blue'. He is methodical in handling the crisps 'between forefinger and thumb'. All Beard's actions are precise and deliberate. He leaves nothing to chance.

The most interesting thing about his personality is that he is obsessive. For no apparent reason, he gets caught up in playing mind games with the passenger sitting opposite. Beard has such a weird imagination that he even wonders if he might be sharing a compartment with a 'psychopath'. I get the impression that he is a typical people-watcher.

Examiner's comment

- The opening directly addresses the question, but expression is note-like ('Obsessive. A man who turns everything into a drama').
- Overall discussion is focused clearly on character study.
- Points are clearly stated and well-organised into paragraphs.
- Good use is made of apt reference and quotation.
- Although slightly disjointed, language is lively and fluent throughout. (13/15)

CLASS/HOMEWORK EXERCISE

QUESTION A

(ii) In your opinion, how do Beard's thoughts and actions reveal his attitude towards his fellow passenger? Support your response with reference to the text. (15)

Allow about 12–14 minutes and aim for three focused, supported points in short paragraphs.

Prompt!

- Is Michael Beard worried about how he appears to strangers?
- Does his behaviour suggest a lack of confidence in company?
- Is Beard overly-imaginative?
- Are there signs of fear or even paranoia?
- Does Beard seem confrontational? Resentful? Dismissive?

LESSON 9: ANALYSING TRAVEL WRITING

Learning aim: To analyse key features of successful travel writing

India with Sanjeev Bhaskar

Many travel writers are fascinated by the country of their roots. In this extract from the documentary, India with Sanjeev Bhaskar, *the author describes a lively religious celebration.*

We have arrived in Calcutta at an extraordinary time of year and one that children look especially forward to – Diwali – the Hindu New Year.

This is one of the most important Hindu festivals, as well as the most popular, and is celebrated for five continuous days. It's thought of as a time to celebrate the triumph of good over evil, and hope over darkness.

'Diwali' derives from the Sanskrit word, 'Deepavali'. This literally means the Festival of Light, and a walk through any Indian city, town or village on the night of Diwali will testify to how seriously the people take it. Every available lamp and candle is lit, and the rooftops are a riot of noise and colour as fireworks light up the night sky.

Diwali honours Lakshmi, Goddess of wealth, beauty and prosperity, both material and spiritual. Hindus associate Lakshmi with good fortune and so paying homage to her ensures success for the coming year. As well as the usual rituals and prayers, homes are made as bright as possible to venerate the Goddess.

Candles and *diyas* (little clay lamps) are often out-done by fireworks, electrical displays and neon colours. *Kandils* (bright paper lanterns) are an integral part of Diwali decorations and traditional motifs adorn doorways and courtyards, welcoming Lakshmi into their homes. To indicate her long-awaited arrival, small footprints are often drawn with rice flour and vermilion powder all over the houses. It is believed she visits the brightest, cleanest homes first.

My Diwali experience began at dusk on a suburban rooftop. A hundred families who each live in the neighbouring blocks have come together for their community celebration.

Rockets, roman candles, catherine wheels and fireworks that behave like rudimentary flamethrowers are all lit and tossed haphazardly. Men, women and children all jostle to light the touchpaper. There's no organised display here; indeed there's no organisation whatsoever. The proximity of the people to the fireworks themselves is one worry as at times you can't tell them apart and I'm sure those beautiful, undulating silk saris aren't fire resistant. Nevertheless, the collective bravado carries the day and the young children dance, point and laugh with delight. Multi-coloured sparks blaze against the night sky.

QUESTION A

(iii) What features of the writer's style make this an interesting piece of travel writing? Support your answer by close reference to the text. (20)

Sample answer

Sanjeev Bhaskar gives a powerful impression of this Hindu festival. First, he provides background facts so that we know exactly what the celebration means – 'literally the Festival of Light'. He tells readers that the celebrations continue for five days of 'rituals and prayers'. This would be helpful to tourists in the same way as explaining to visitors what Christmas in Ireland means to many Irish people.

The writer also takes us along with him on his journey through Calcutta by introducing us to the community there. Diwali is clearly an important religious event. Over a hundred local families have come together to welcome in the Hindu New Year. Bhaskar emphasises how candles, lanterns and fireworks are to be found everywhere – 'Men, women and children all jostle to light the touchpaper'. We can imagine the drama of chaotic scenes ('there's no organisation whatsoever') as he seems equally entertained and frightened by the flamethrowers.

Vivid descriptions bring this colourful place to life. The exciting mood is created by the wonderful image: 'young children dance, point and laugh with delight' and by dynamic verbs: 'tossed', 'jostle' and 'blaze'. We get a flavour of the importance of Diwali without any persuasion from the writer who keeps an open mind about Indian culture. The extract draws us in because most people are intrigued by the exotic aspects of foreign places.

Bhaskar himself is obviously fascinated by India. He has a good eye for colourful detail. We are left in no doubt that he is passionate about the country of his roots. He notices everything and is keen to invite readers to explore Calcutta with him.

Examiner's comment

- A well-supported top-grade response that never loses touch with the question.
- The reader's experience is central to the discussion ('we know exactly what the celebration means').
- Includes strong points on atmosphere ('drama of chaotic scenes') and the writer's use of descriptive language ('wonderful image', 'dynamic verbs').
- References range widely to illustrate the qualities of effective travel writing.
- The expression is varied, fluent and controlled throughout ('The extract draws us in because most people are intrigued by the exotic aspects of foreign places'). (20/20)

Moscow Weekend

In the following Urban Travel Blog *extract, Laura Gozzi describes a visit to the Russian capital.*

RSS 

If you've never travelled to Russia, you're probably struggling to imagine what Moscow is like, and if you know more than one person who has been, the chances are that you have heard extremely conflicting opinions about it.

Throughout the Cold War, Moscow used to be the capital of the 'other' world, the home of lofty ideals and harsh realities; today, many young Muscovites would rather talk about the city's craft beer revolution than the Bolshevik one.

But Moscow's strange charm remains. More often than not, the city doesn't seem to make any sense: blonde girls in white furs and shiny leather boots stroll around the stalls in neighbourhood markets, buying cottage cheese and honey from old, toothless, dark-skinned Armenian men; the glitzy windows of Western clothes shops reflect the enormous, grey, terrifying façades of old Soviet government buildings.

And in the midst of it all there is you, the visitor – the latest addition to a city that has never stopped growing and changing, carrying with it more history than one can imagine. Maybe that's why there has never been a better time to visit Moscow: the eclectic mix of old, new and timeless makes it a truly unique destination that is neither Europe nor Asia, but on the cusp of both – retaining an air of chaotic vastness, frenzied life and bustling exhilaration. Moscow is likely to surprise, shock and seduce you. Get ready.

Walking around Moscow is not unlike skipping from one century to the next; the walls, streets and homes of the city are soaked in history, translating into a huge variety of attractions that reflect all strands of Russia's convoluted past.

With its fiery red Historical Museum, the majestic Kremlin, the colourful domes of St Basil's cathedral and the sparkle of the gigantic, 19th century shopping centre, Red Square is a sight to behold. The Kremlin complex is home to a host of churches, museums and government buildings, but the visit can be expensive and time-consuming because of the infinite queues at the ticket office.

CLASS/HOMEWORK EXERCISE

QUESTION A

(iii) What features of the writer's style make this an engaging and informative piece of travel writing? Support your answer by close reference to the text. (20)

Allow about 15–18 minutes and aim for at least three focused, supported points.

Prompt!

- Comment on the opening. Is the language accessible?
- Check the tone. Relaxed? Personal? Inviting? Informal?
- What interesting details and facts are provided?
- Do contrasting images illustrate and enliven the writing?
- How does the writer create a vivid sense of place?
- Which words or phrases convey the writer's experience?
- Is the piece overly-enthusiastic or balanced and realistic?

LESSON 10: ANALYSING SETTING

Learning aim: To analyse and discuss key aspects of setting

Wuthering Heights

Emily Brontë's only novel, Wuthering Heights, *was published in 1847 and is widely considered a classic of English literature. The setting is a remote area in the harsh and isolated Yorkshire moors. At the beginning of the story, Mr Lockwood (who is renting a local property) visits Wuthering Heights, the home of his landlord, Mr Heathcliff.*

Read the following extract carefully, paying particular attention to how the writer creates a sense of place.

Wuthering Heights is the name of Mr. Heathcliff's dwelling. 'Wuthering' being a significant provincial adjective, descriptive of the atmospheric tumult to which its station is exposed in stormy weather. Pure, bracing ventilation they must have up there at all times, indeed; one may guess the power of the north wind blowing over the edge, by the excessive slant of a few stunted firs at the end of the house; and by a range of gaunt thorns all stretching their limbs one way, as if craving alms of the sun.

Happily, the architect had foresight to build it strong: the narrow windows are deeply set in the wall, and the corners defended with large jutting stones.

Before passing the threshold, I paused to admire a quantity of grotesque[1] carving lavished over the front, and especially about the principal door; above which, among a wilderness of crumbling griffins[2] and shameless little boys, I detected the date '1500', and the name 'Hareton Earnshaw'. I would have made a few comments, and requested a short history of the place from the surly owner; but his attitude at the door appeared to demand my speedy entrance, or complete departure, and I had no desire to aggravate his impatience previous to inspecting the penetralium.[3]

One step brought us into the family sitting-room, without any introductory lobby or passage: they call it here 'the house' pre-eminently. It includes kitchen and parlour, generally; but I believe at Wuthering Heights the kitchen is forced to retreat altogether into another quarter: at least I distinguished a chatter of tongues, and a clatter of culinary utensils, deep within; and I observed no signs of roasting, boiling, or baking, about the huge fireplace; nor any glitter of copper saucepans and tin cullenders on the walls. One end, indeed, reflected splendidly both light and heat from ranks of immense pewter dishes, interspersed with silver jugs and tankards, towering row after row, on a vast oak dresser, to the very roof. The latter had never been underdrawn:[4] its entire anatomy lay bare to an inquiring eye, except where a frame of wood laden with oatcakes and clusters of legs of beef, mutton, and ham, concealed it.

Above the chimney were sundry[5] villainous old guns, and a couple of horse-pistols: and, by way of ornament, three gaudily-painted canisters disposed along its ledge. The floor was of smooth, white stone; the chairs, high-backed, primitive structures, painted green: one or two heavy black ones lurking in the shade. In an arch under the dresser reposed a huge, liver-coloured bitch pointer, surrounded by a swarm of squealing puppies; and other dogs haunted other recesses.

1. Repulsive, distorted
2. Mythical beasts, half-eagle and half-lion
3. Inner part of a building
4. Covered on the inside
5. Various

Some stylistic features

◆ **Narrative voice** ◆ **Detailed description** ◆ **Imagery and symbolism**

- Brontë's use of narrative voice (through Mr Lockwood) introduces readers to a seemingly uncivilised world. Yet Lockwood appears to be intrigued by the hostile atmosphere he finds in Heathcliff's house.
- Throughout the extract, detailed description adds a vivid visual quality to the remote farmhouse.
- Effective imagery reveals interesting aspects of both the exterior and interior of the house – and of its owner.

Close analysis of Emily Brontë's language provides an understanding of the extract and is essential for answering questions successfully. The following discussion notes focus on key words and phrases that illustrate the writer's skill at creating setting.

From the start, the strong sense of isolation and restlessness provoked by the setting contributes to the novel's tone. Situated in the **harsh and desolate moors** of Yorkshire, Wuthering Heights is inhospitable and fortress-like, as if built for defence: 'The narrow windows are deeply set into the wall, and the corners defended with large jutting stones'. Mr Heathcliff, the owner, is 'surly'.

Brontë makes use of a familiar literary technique, known as **pathetic fallacy**. This involves associating nature – particularly the weather – with the emotions of characters. We are told that Wuthering Heights is as wild and windswept as it sounds. Lockwood notes that the adjective 'wuthering' is an apt description of 'the atmospheric tumult to which its station is exposed in stormy weather'. These references might imply that Heathcliff may also have an uncontrollable personality.

Lockwood imagines the fierce 'north wind' blowing around the bleak building, causing the 'stunted fir trees' to bend. The imagery is unsettling and immediately conveys a disturbing sense of distortion and disfigurement in nature. The ghostly **personification** indicates helplessness and desperation: 'gaunt thorns all stretching their limbs one way, as if craving alms of the sun'.

The interior atmosphere is equally inhospitable. Wuthering Heights is an uninviting, functional place with 'a quantity of grotesque carving' and other 'primitive structures'. Everything is utilitarian – and sometimes intimidating. Several 'villainous old guns' are displayed above Heathcliff's fireplace and the room is 'haunted' by vicious dogs. The gothic darkness and strangeness of Brontë's setting creates an instant **sense of mystery** that makes us want to read on.

CLASS/HOMEWORK EXERCISE

QUESTION A

(iii) Based on what you have read in the above extract from *Wuthering Heights*, do you agree that Emily Brontë skilfully evokes a strong sense of place and atmosphere? Support your answer with reference to the text. (20)

Allow about 15–18 minutes and aim for at least three focused points. The notes above will be helpful in responding to the question.

LESSON 11: AUTOBIOGRAPHICAL WRITING

Learning aim: To analyse and understand key aspects of autobiographical writing

Unreliable Memoirs

In this abridged extract from his autobiography Unreliable Memoirs, *Clive James describes his schooldays in Australia.*

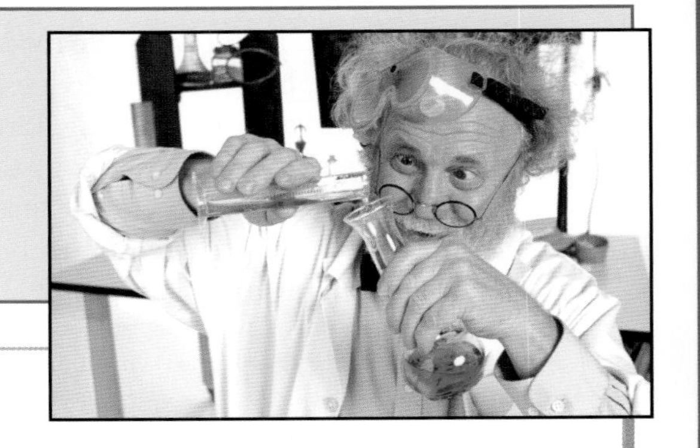

1. In that first year the only thing that made me worth knowing was my good marks. The teachers weren't brilliant but they were conscientious. At the half-yearly examinations I averaged in the high nineties, coming third in the class. Things might have gone on like that for a good while longer if it had not been for Mary Luke.

2. I was coping with physics and chemistry well enough while Mr Ryan was still teaching them. But Mr Ryan was due for retirement, an event which was hastened by an accident in the laboratory. He was showing us how careful you had to be when handling potassium in the presence of water. Certainly you had to be more careful than he was. The school's entire supply of potassium was ignited at once. Wreathed by dense smoke and lit by garish flames, the stunned Mr Ryan looked like an ancient Greek god in receipt of bad news. The smoke enveloped us all. Windows being thrown open, it jetted into what passed for a playground, where it hung around like some sinister leftover from a battle on the Somme. Shocked, scorched and gassed, Mr Ryan was carried away, never to return.

3. Back from his third retirement came Mary Luke. A chronic shortage of teachers led to Mary Luke being magically resurrected after each burial. Why he should have been called Mary was lost in antiquity. The school presented him with a pocket watch every time he retired. Perhaps that was a mistake. It might have been the massed ticking that kept him alive. Anyway, Mary Luke, having ruined science for a whole generation of schoolboys, came back from the shadows to ruin science for me.

4. Mary was keen but incomprehensible. The first thing he said at the beginning of every lesson, whether of physics or chemistry, was 'Make a Bunsen burner'. He was apparently convinced that given the right encouragement we would continue our science studies in makeshift laboratories at home. So we might have done, if we could have understood anything else he said. The mouth moved constantly. 'Combustioff off magnesioff,' Mary would announce keenly. 'Magensioff off oxidoff off hydrogoff off givoff off.' Worriedly I slid the cap off the inverted jar and ignited the gaseous contents to prove the hydrogoff had been givoff off. Carefully I drew the apparatus in my book, already aware that these experiments would be the last I would ever understand.

5. In English I shone – fitfully, but sufficiently to keep my morale from collapsing altogether. Our teacher in the early years was 'Jazz' Aked. He also doubled as our music teacher: hence the nickname. 'Jazz' taught English according to the curriculum. Without resorting to violence, 'Jazz' had a way of getting results. Eventually I learned to parse any sentence[1] I was given. I couldn't do it now, but the knowledge is still there somewhere at an unconscious level. It was invaluable training. On top of that, he set good essay subjects. My essays were sometimes read out to the class. I was thereby established all over again as teacher's pet, but at least it was something, in those dreadful days when everyone else seemed to be doubling in size overnight, while simultaneously acquiring an Adam's apple like a half-swallowed rock.

1. Identify words and their grammatical functions

Autobiographical writing skills

- Personal record of thoughts and feelings
- Reader gains insights into the writer's character
- Describe people and places in detail
- Use descriptive and imaginative language
- Include a reflective tone
- Write in the first person

Close analysis of Clive James's language provides a greater understanding of the extract. The following discussion notes focus on key words and phrases that illustrate James's autobiographical skills.

Paragraph 1 provides a build-up to the entertaining **anecdote** about Mary Luke. Readers are led to expect that something dramatic is about to happen. The writer's tone is self-deprecating – he was 'coping' with science subjects.

Through the use of **understatement**, Clive James introduces the 'accident in the laboratory'. The explosion is treated humorously. It's highly ironic that Mr Ryan almost kills himself while demonstrating 'how careful you had to be when handling potassium'. Amid the chaos of the scene, the injured teacher is cleverly portrayed as a war victim ('Shocked, scorched and gassed').

The comic description of the mysteriously-named Mary Luke depends largely on **exaggeration** to illustrate his eccentricity. The teacher's strange pronunciation turns him into the stereotypical mad scientist.

Paragraph 5 gives us an insight into the writer's relief that he was good at '*something*'. James's **confidential tone** is revealing. As a writer looking back on his school English classes, he values the importance of learning about grammar ('invaluable training'). The extract reveals several aspects of the writer's personality. He is very perceptive with a good sense of humour, but also has a serious side to his character.

QUESTION A

(iii) Based on your reading of the extract above, do you agree that Clive James's account of his schooldays is both entertaining and well observed. (20)

Sample answer

This is a lively and amusing piece of autobiographical writing. Clive James has obvious skills in bringing his schooldays to life. He relives that memorable day in Mr Ryan's class when things went badly wrong. The detailed description of the disastrous science experiment adds realism. I can just imagine the chaos as the lab is filled with 'dense smoke and lit by garish flames'.

The writer's sarcastic tone is also engaging. Mary Luke should clearly not be anywhere near a classroom, but keeps reappearing in the school 'magically resurrected after each burial'. What makes this teacher funny is that he is so keen and his 'mouth moved constantly'. Unfortunately, he is completely incomprehensible.

James creates closely observed characters throughout this enjoyable piece. Mary Luke's ridiculous speech makes him a larger than life figure. By contrast, 'Jazz' Aked seems quite normal. We get an understanding into his natural ability to teach when the writer casually says that Jazz could do this without 'resorting to violence'.

Such insights are typical of Clive James's insightful style. All through the extract, he allows us to see him both as a young student and also as a grown-up reflecting on past experiences. The final paragraph is more serious and personal. I could imagine the awkward young teenager who was secretly proud of being the 'teacher's pet'. His own lack of confidence is evident at the end.

Examiner's comment

- Well-focused answer that addresses the question directly.
- Impressive points on the writer's approach ('sarcastic tone'), character sketches ('closely observed characters') and personal insights ('I could imagine the awkward young teenager').
- Well-structured and organised into effective paragraphs.
- Expression is varied, controlled and succinct, and key points are aptly supported with carefully selected quotations.
- A very successful response. (20/20)

CLASS/HOMEWORK EXERCISE

QUESTION A

(iii) Imagine that you are working on your autobiography. Write two paragraphs describing a memorable experience during your time in National School. (20)

Allow about 15–18 minutes and aim for 180–200 words.

Prompt!

- An autobiography tells the story of the writer's life. When you are using an autobiographical style, avoid the trap of routinely telling your life story chronologically with dates and places in order. Instead of including all the boring details, aim for a lively personal memoir that is both entertaining and interesting.
- Successful memoirs are usually reflective in tone and can sometimes be nostalgic (viewing the past sentimentally). Writers often use anecdotes to add interest. An anecdote is a short account of a particular incident or event that readers might find amusing or thought-provoking.

LESSON 12: VISUAL LITERACY 1

Learning aim: To improve visual literacy and write effectively about visual texts

The Leaving Certificate English Syllabus envisages the subject 'English' as 'not limited to the written word' (Leaving Certificate Syllabus, English, para. 2.6) and it identifies the importance of visual literacy.

Visual texts (photographs, book covers, posters, paintings, screenshots, graphics, etc.) are usually included as part of the Comprehending A questions.

Visual literacy is the ability to understand, interpret, decode, question and find meaning from information presented in the form of images.

You might be asked to:

- Write a description of an image or series of images.
- Analyse and interpret images and their effectiveness.
- Compare two or more visuals.
- Comment on the impact visual images make on you.
- Write an introduction to a group of images.
- Relate the visual imagery to an accompanying written text.
- Suggest alternative images to illustrate a text effectively.

Since meaning can be communicated effectively through the visual medium, images can therefore be 'read'.

STUDYING VISUAL IMAGES

▶ **Consider the purpose**

Is it to inform? Persuade? Entertain? Educate? Shock?

▶ **Examine the subject matter**

Who or what is the subject of the visual? What details are included?

▶ **Comment on visual features**

How effective is the use of colour, contrasts and symbols? Do they enhance the picture's message?

▶ **Assess the tone or atmosphere**

Does the image create a particular mood? Does it tell a story or convey a message?

▶ **Think about the impact on the viewer**

What is the effect of the image?

▶ **Study the most striking visual elements**

What strikes you most about an image at first glance? It could be the mix of settings; characters, their expressions; use of light and shadow, camera angles, etc.

Close analysis of a visual image is essential for answering questions successfully. The following discussion notes focus on some key aspects of the composition of this photo of the actress Saoirse Ronan.

Everything about the image reflects the **celebratory mood** of the occasion – a famous Irish star poses for photographers after receiving another film award.

The **background** logo for the BIFA (British Independent Film Awards) provides information and a context for the photograph.

Saoirse Ronan is the subject of the image and is the focal point – literally the centre of attention here. Her appearance, jewellery, etc. suggest the formality and glamour of the event.

- The **purpose** of the picture is to show a successful young actress.
- Saoirse's dark dress provides a **contrast** to the pale background.
- The celebrity's relaxed, confident **facial expression** reveals her satisfaction at winning.
- **The props** (film award and champagne bottle) add to the party atmosphere.
- It could be argued that such **staged** photographs lack spontaneity and originality.

CLASS/HOMEWORK EXERCISE

QUESTION A

(i) Write a personal response to the image below, commenting on the aspects of the photograph that make most impact on you. (15)

Allow about 12–14 minutes and aim for three focused, supported points in short paragraphs.

Prompt!

- What does the picture to the right show?
- Did the image have an emotive effect on you?
- Are there interesting details included?
- What does the young woman's body language suggest?
- How important is the hand-written sign?
- What message does the picture convey?
- Is the photo entirely convincing?

LESSON 13: VISUAL LITERACY 2

Learning aim: To compare visual images and write effectively about visual features

'READING' A VISUAL TEXT

To read a visual text, you must view the text closely. Work out the main idea and how the **visual codes** work. Think about the purpose of the text and how these techniques help to communicate a message to the audience.

Elements include camera angle, lighting, special effects, layout, dominant image, symbols, patterns, colour, font, graphic, contrast, etc.

The photographer uses the camera to construct the **message** he or she wants to communicate. In order to 'read' the photograph, it is important to consider the purpose and recognise the techniques that have been used. Critical literacy depends on asking questions as well as analysing images.

Is the main purpose of the image to inform? Persuade? Entertain? Challenge? Some photographs can create an emotional response. Others convey meaning and provoke a response. Images can also be **aesthetically pleasing**. These will appeal to our appreciation of beauty or artistic expression.

Prompt!

- Look closely at the colours and layout.
- What colours are used? How are they used? Do they portray different moods or personalities? Are colours used as symbols?
- Predominantly bright colours and 'busy' layout may promise excitement. More subtle colours and conservative layout may appeal to traditional values.
- Divide an image into thirds from the top and sides and check the placement of people and/or objects. It's likely that anyone or anything in the top section is more empowered than in the bottom third.

QUESTION A

(ii) Which of the following images do you think best illustrates today's younger generation? [You might consider the subject matter, setting, mood, body language, props, photographic qualities, etc.] (15)

Sample answer

Image 2 gives the most positive view of young people. The photograph showing a group of young people on graduation day has a very dynamic feel. Their arms are outstretched as they throw their academic caps in the air. They all seem to be flying high and this captures their sense of achievement.

The photo conveys their mood of optimism cleverly as they appear to be almost dancing on air. To me, this shows that our generation is lively, intelligent, ambitious and hard-working. These five young students – male and female – are typical of the great majority who are determined to make their mark on the world.

Among several effective symbols in this dramatic image are clear blue skies and strong body language – both of which emphasise what is best about today's youth. Far too often, newspapers publish pictures that give a negative view. This picture is the opposite, clearly showing youthful idealism as the new graduates reach for the sky.

Examiner's comment

- Focused, confident response directly tackling the question.
- Clearly organised points supported by apt reference throughout.
- Discusses particular visual features, such as colour and symbolism.
- Expression is controlled and fluent. (15/15)

CLASS/HOMEWORK EXERCISE

QUESTION A

(ii) Select one of the three visual images above for a newspaper article entitled 'Youth Culture'. Support your answer with reference to your chosen image.

[You might consider the subject matter, setting, mood, photographic qualities, etc.] (15)

Allow about 12–14 minutes and aim for three focused, supported points in short paragraphs.

LESSON 14: VISUAL LITERACY 3

Learning aim: To analyse the impact of contrasting visual images

Visual Literacy is an important 21st century skill. Today we are bombarded with images, advertisements, cartoons, charts, collages, comic books, icons, and websites, etc. It is important, therefore, that we are able to interpret, recognise, appreciate and understand information presented through images.

STUDYING VISUAL IMAGES

As readers, we make observations, connections and inferences about what the creator of the image is trying to do and the image's significance.

1. What do I see? (Consider the people, objects and activities in images.)
2. What is the image-maker's purpose? (Is it to analyse, move, persuade, express, document, entertain?)
3. What reactions or questions does the image raise in my mind?

CLASS/HOMEWORK EXERCISE

Read the following text and answer the question that follows.

During World War II, Bruce Chatwin stayed with his grandparents who had a curiosity cabinet that fascinated him. Among the items it contained was a 'piece of brontosaurus' sent to his grandmother by her cousin Charles Milward. He had discovered the remains in a cave in Chilean Patagonia. The skin inspired Chatwin decades later to visit Patagonia, and resulted in his travel book, *In Patagonia*.

IN PATAGONIA

In my grandmother's dining-room there was a glass-fronted cabinet and in the cabinet a piece of skin. It was a small piece only, but thick and leathery, with strands of coarse, reddish hair. It was stuck to a card with a rusty pin. On the card was some writing in faded black ink, but I was too young then to read.

'What's that?'

'A piece of brontosaurus.'

My mother knew the names of two prehistoric animals, the brontosaurus and the mammoth. She knew it was not a mammoth. Mammoths come from Siberia.

The brontosaurus, I learned, was an animal that had drowned in the Flood, being too big for Noah to ship aboard the Ark. I pictured a shaggy, lumbering creature with claws and fangs, and a malicious green light in its eyes. Sometimes the brontosaurus would crash through the bedroom wall and wake me from my sleep.

This particular brontosaurus had lived in Patagonia, a country in South America, at the far end of the world. Thousands of years before, it had fallen into a glacier, travelled down a mountain of blue ice, and arrived in perfect condition at the bottom. Here my grandmother's cousin, Charley Milward the Sailor, found it.

Directly he saw the brontosaurus poking out of the ice, he knew what he had to do. He had it jointed, salted, packed in barrels and shipped to the Natural History Museum in South Kensington. I pictured blood and ice, flesh and salt, gangs of Indian workmen and lines of barrels along a shore – a work of giants and all to no purpose; the brontosaurus went rotten on its voyage through the tropics and arrived in London a putrefied mess which was why you saw brontosaurus bones in the museum, but no skin.

Fortunately, cousin Charley had posted a scrap to my grandmother.

QUESTION A

(ii) In your opinion, based on the written text above, how effectively do the two book covers (Image A and Image B) illustrate the appeal of Patagonia? Support your answer with detailed reference to both covers and to the written text. (20)

Allow about 12–14 minutes and aim for three focused, supported points in your answer.

Image A

Image B

Sample answer

Book cover B illustrates the attraction of Patagonia more effectively than image A. While image A is modern and artistic with its parallel lines conveying the country's natural beauty, I feel it lacks any real punch.

The varying shades of blue reflect the skies and glaciers of the region, the green shows the emptiness and the earth colours suggest ancient places with their buried remains, yet it does not adequately capture the allure of this vast country.

The second image (B) uses dramatic contrast of light and shade in its dynamic picture of the country. Immediately, we are reminded of the mystery of this largely uninhabited country. I could imagine Chatwin standing looking at this scene. He had been intrigued by it as a child, from the first glimpse of the 'thick and leathery' piece of skin which his cousin had sent home.

What else lay hidden in the still lake? I thought the purple mountain ranges in the distance gave an impression of the vast scale of a land just waiting to be explored.

Capitals used in the B title give a sense of importance, unlike the type in image A. The recommendation by Paul Theroux also emphasises the energy of the travel experience, and this is increased by the alliterative phrase, 'BOISTEROUS, AND BIZARRE'. Image B more successively catches the excitement awaiting the reader in this famous travel book.

Examiner's comment

- Some excellent analysis of the visual qualities of both covers.
- Relevant, focused points supported effectively by suitable reference
- Discussion ranges widely, contrasting colours, typeface and dramatic impact.
- Expression is very impressive throughout, e.g. 'it does not adequately capture the allure of this vast country'. (15/15)

CLASS/HOMEWORK EXERCISE

QUESTION A

(iii) Imagine that you are to give a talk to your class about Bruce Chatwin's book, *In Patagonia*. Which two of the three images below would you choose to use as a backdrop? Explain your choice, discussing the impact you think both of your chosen images would make on your audience.

In your answer, you should refer both to your chosen visual images and to Chatwin's written text. (20)

Allow about 15–18 minutes and aim for at least three focused, supported points in your response.

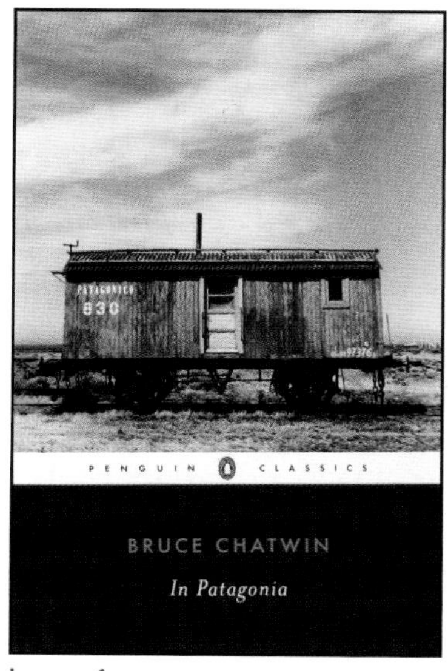

Image 1

Image 2

Image 3

COMPREHENDING B

COMPREHENDING B

Functional writing asks you to write for a specific, practical reason. You are likely to write in a particular format, such as a talk, letter, email, diary, proposal, blog, editorial, speech, magazine article, introduction, interview, report, review, etc.

The Comprehending B question is awarded 50 marks.

For each particular task, it is essential to use the **appropriate register** (language, tone and lay-out).

You should aim for 450–500 words (usually five or six paragraphs written over 35–40 minutes).

Marking Scheme

Purpose: Are all aspects of the task being addressed? (15 marks)

Coherence: Is the response controlled, paragraphed and sustained throughout? (15 marks)

Language: Is the writing appropriate to the task (register, fluency, punctuation)? (15 marks)

Mechanics: Are spellings and grammar accurate? (5 marks)

To define a Comprehending B task, consider the following:

- What do I have to write about? (content)
- Who am I as writer/speaker? (persona)
- For whom am I writing? (audience)
- Why am I writing this? (purpose)
- What type of language and tone will I use? (register)
- What format should the writing take? (genre and structure)

LESSON 15: SHORT TALK

Learning aim: To present a clear point of view in a persuasive w

Comprehending Question B tasks frequently include writing the text of a short talk or presentation. A talk is usually less formal than a persuasive speech. The purpose, audience and persona of the writer will all suggest the register or tone.

The content and register will depend on whether the talk is meant to be informative, reflective, persuasive or descriptive. Talks are often a mix of argument and persuasion and can also include elements of other language styles, such as descriptive and narrative writing.

You might be asked, for example, to write a short talk (or speech) welcoming a well-known person to your school. The tone in that case will be very different to a talk to your classmates about an important issue that affects young people.

QUESTION B

Write the text of a talk you would deliver to your class in which you reflect on the pressures experienced by young people today and how they cope with these demands. (50)

Allow about 35–40 minutes and aim for at least 450 words.

Prompt!

- Planning is essential to producing a successful response. Study the wording of the question and define the task, deciding on the stance or approach.
- Ask yourself the following questions:
- **What do I have to write about?** The demands on young people today and how they respond to these stresses. (Two aspects)
- **Who am I as the writer?** A student.
- **For whom am I writing?** My class.
- **Why am I writing this?** To consider how negative or positive are the demands on young people today and their responses to these pressures. (Stance: agree and/or disagree.)
- **What format should it be?** A talk.
- **What type of language will I use?** Informal, persuasive with a touch of humour.

Draft Structure

Paragraph 1: Introduction

Paragraph 2: Parents

Paragraph 3: Digital era

Paragraph 4: Celebrity image

Paragraph 5: Conclusion

Sample Question B Talk

1. Good morning... We teenagers today face a barrage of demands, global and local, some good, others bad, but all blowing straight towards us as we negotiate our way to adulthood. We all know the difficulty of being different, we are all individuals, and yet we strive hard to be the same, we want to fit in and be respected by our peers. So, do we show our individuality by looking like everyone else? Confusing! Parental expectations, the ever-expanding technology scene and the desire to fit in all seek to shape us as we make our way in this increasingly complex society.

2. Parents seek to influence us from our earliest years. Their worries are fuelled by alarming articles and programmes about teenage problems. They have a new tool in their armour to protect, the text message! Walking home from school, I am interrupted by a tsunami of text messages from my alarmed parent. Where are you? Who are you with? When will you be home? But as a teenager, I crave freedom, the freedom to be me and do what I want to do. I don't want the negative effect of an over-protective parent trying to save me by smothering me in ever increasing circles of protection. I do want a parent to stand by my side as I save myself.

3. Our generation is the first to go through their entire teen years with such a range of digital platforms to inform, entertain and connect with others. Social media sites were formed to enable people keep in touch with ease. But Facebook and Instagram have become 'competition' sites as the numbers of 'likes' one gets are eagerly counted. These sites become addictive and can have a negative effect. Some teens actually wake up during the night to check their profiles. We all know we check our mobiles the moment we first open one eye. As the great actor Orson Welles once remarked, 'I hate television. I hate it as much as peanuts. But I can't stop eating peanuts.'

4. The abundance of celebrity images, photoshopped to perfection, make many teens believe that everyone is better, prettier, skinnier, funnier than they are. One friend of mine posted a picture of herself from the Debs' Ball and said, 'I can't look at myself without wishing I was someone else'. Yet we know that fashion models weigh 23% less than the average female. There is no such thing as 'perfect'. Refuse to accept this negative pressure. Anyway who are the judges of 'perfect' and why should we listen to them?

5. One of my classmates told me if you don't know something, Google it, if you don't know someone, Facebook it and if you can't find something shout: 'Mum!' But I prefer to look on life as a camera. Focus on what's important. Capture the good times. If things don't work out, take another shot! Remember... Be yourself. Everyone else is taken! Thanks for listening.

Examiner's comment

- A successful top-grade response.
- This well-structured talk addresses several aspects of the pressures on young people, including the role played by parents, celebrities, digital and technological advances – and their impact.
- The relaxed but reflective tone is appropriate to an informal talk and there is a clear sense of engagement with the audience. This is shown by use of direct address at the beginning and end of the talk but also throughout the body of the talk, 'Be yourself, everyone else is taken'. (48/50)

GRADE: H1

P = 15/15

C = 14/15

L = 14/15

M = 5/5

TOTAL = 48/50

SUCCESSFUL ANSWERING

How do I write a good opening paragraph?

The purpose of an opening paragraph in a talk is to engage the listeners, make them aware of the direction of the talk (the approach or stance) and let them know briefly what is about to be covered. Aim to get the attention of your listener or reader with the opening sentence. Think of it as a hook, drawing in the reader. An interesting quotation, definition or curious fact can often be effective. Short dramatic questions can also be useful.

Rhetorical skills

A rhetorical question is a question asked for effect; its main purpose is to engage the audience, it does not require an answer. For example:

Statement: *A name is not important.*

Rhetorical question: *What's in a name?*

Techniques of persuasive writing include:

- Gaining audience attention from the start
- Maintaining interest by engaging the audience
- Use of emotive language to show empathy
- Rhetorical devices, such as repetition and questions
- Personal anecdotes and humour

Comprehending B

CLASS/HOMEWORK EXERCISE

QUESTION B

Imagine that you are a refugee who has recently been granted asylum in Ireland. Write the text of a talk you would deliver to a group of young people, explaining why you chose to come here and discussing some of the positive and negative aspects of life in Ireland since your arrival. (50)

Allow about 35–40 minutes and aim for at least 450 words.

To put forward a persuasive and compelling argument, the speaker has to make a positive impression on the audience.

LESSON 16: PERSUASIVE WRITING

Learning aim: To write an engaging and persuasive talk

The Opinion Piece

In this newspaper article, Karlin Lillington argues that dogs make the best domestic pets.

'Oh my. Are they all yours? How do you manage?'

My partner and I rarely complete a leisurely amble around the local park without getting stopped at least once by strangers. Sometimes they have one or two of their own.

Occasionally, just for the fun of watching a face morph from startled to alarmed in a nanosecond, I'll cheerfully reply, 'And there are even more at home.'

Dogs, of course. Dogs.

Big ones and small ones. Fluffy ones and smooth ones. Elderly ones, elegantly grey muzzled and browed, as hard of hearing as an old codger on a corner stool in a pub. Young ones that chase dilapidated tennis balls into the sea and relish a stinking piece of dried tripe[1] the way a connoisseur would sniff and happily sigh over a glass of vintage Lynch-Bages.[2]

Some people have one or two. We have . . . well, let me see. Currently seven, down from 10 just over a year ago (the heartbreaking side of having a gang of much-loved seniors, so wonderfully full of character in their dotage but on limited retirement time). We also have a foster dog (what's one more?).

We love dogs. We like cats, yes (we have three), but we love dogs. We both grew up with them.

I refer to us as the Brady Bunch of Dogs, even though he brought one to the relationship and I brought, er, four. Then it was five. Then six. All Cavalier King Charles spaniels, most of them rescue dogs. (Since I set up Irish Cavalier Rescue, more than a decade ago, we have taken in and re-homed a couple of hundred little cavaliers.)

When we realised that we had a house full of ageing but moderately active dogs – an incongruous mix of Alsatians and cavaliers – we knew it was time to add a youngster. (Wouldn't you?) Of course – long hairy story short – one became two. And, fulfilling a decades-long wish of mine, they are Pyrenean mountain dogs, a collective, deep-woofing, goofy yet regal 200-plus pounds of them.

So there's hair. (We've a Dyson and a Miele[3] forming a laughable defence.) There are muddy paws, sea-wet body shakes, the occasional indoor accident (that's what tile floors are for), cacophonous[4] barking from cavaliers wanting breakfast, hopeful demands for ball throwing from the Alsatian, and acres of outstretched sleeping Pyreneans, like deep-breathing polar-bear rugs.

When we needed a new car we brought an extra-large cage around to the dealerships, to measure the interiors for multiple-dog transport, and chose a model based on optimum canine capacity (a Hyundai Santa Fe).

I cannot imagine a home without a dog. That's merely a house. A sterile, hair-free, too-quiet, wagless desert, lacking pink tummies waiting to be rubbed and a row of earnest fuzzy faces peering out of the front window, waiting for your return.

Dogs are just the best. The merry, devoted, intelligent, humorous, empathetic, forgiving best.

1. Stomach lining of an animal
2. French wine
3. Vacuum cleaners
4. Loud and discordant

A cat is a noble friend, indeed, and completes a home in a different way. But dogs! Only dogs provide that unique form of joyful yet meditative companionship as you traverse the moors or a beach.

Ever loyal, they wake each day ready for whatever you want to do. Every day is a perfect start for them, full of promise, adventure, friendship, silliness. And you. They are a daily reminder of how to live a good life.

That's why dogs are the best. And why I agree with the American cowboy humorist and actor Will Rogers, who said: 'If there are no dogs in heaven, then when I die I want to go where they went.'

Me too. And, hey, dogs: I'll have tennis balls and dried tripe chews when I get there.

SOME PERSUASIVE WRITING FEATURES

- **Personal engaging tone**
- **Humorous touches**
- **Lively illustrations**
- **Emotive language**
- **Repetition, short sentences**

Close analysis of Karlin Lillington's language provides a greater understanding of the extract and is essential for answering questions successfully. The following discussion notes focus on key words and phrases that illustrate Lillington's persuasive writing skills.

The writer's snappy introduction immediately attracts the reader's attention. Karlin Lillington's use of a question creates a small **dramatic scene**. The phrase 'all yours' adds further interest. Does it refer to children? Shopping bags? We can imagine how strangers might react to her when they see her walking several dogs in the park.

The conversational language is in keeping with the writer's **informal tone** and sense of humour, which is evident in the mischievous delight taken in observing people's faces ('startled to alarmed'). The list of dogs is also light-hearted, particularly as some of them are described in human terms.

Lillington explains her love of dogs and makes a number of compelling **points** about why they are the best pets. Some are 'full of character', they provide 'companionship' and are 'Ever loyal'.

Short sentences emphasise the writer's enthusiastic views – 'We love dogs', 'So there's hair'. Repetition is frequently used for the same purpose; dogs enjoy lives of 'promise, adventure, friendship, silliness'.

Throughout the piece, Lillington takes a **personal approach** always inviting us into her confidence. While some of the language is emotive ('Dogs are just the best'), it is never sentimental. The little inclusive asides, such as 'Wouldn't you?' are presented in brackets and make a direct appeal to readers, encouraging us to agree with her views.

The final **quotation** from a famous American dog-lover is typically entertaining and easy-going. Without using obvious arguments, the writer has illustrated how dogs can enrich everyday life. The reference back to 'dried tripe' rounds off the article effectively.

CLASS/HOMEWORK EXERCISE

QUESTION B

You have been asked to give a talk to your class entitled 'Dogs do not make good household pets'. Write the text of the talk you would deliver. (50)

Allow about 35–40 minutes and aim for at least 450 words.

Prompt!

- Aim to persuade the audience to your viewpoint by conveying your opinions clearly and confidently.
- Be careful not to overdo the emotional appeal.
- Make sure that your arguments are as coherent, well-informed and convincing as possible.

Sample opening paragraph

I am a very strong believer in freedom. Not just for people, but for animals as well. In my opinion, if people want toys, they should buy them. If they want companionship, they should seek it with their own kind. Dogs should not be kept indoors for hours while their owners are out working or enjoying themselves. When I'm in school, I often hear poor unfortunate suffering dogs barking non-stop because they have been left abandoned. It's bad enough listening to the teachers howling at us all day, but this makes life worse. Imagine living next door to an unhappy terrier! There are lots of other reasons for not keeping dogs as family pets. They can be violent towards children, they often smell badly and they are usually very expensive to keep.

Examiner's comment

- There is the basis of an effective introductory paragraph here.
- The personal approach engages attention and the initial point about freedom is clearly stated.
- While the reference to 'teachers howling' adds to the informal tone, the mention of 'poor unfortunate suffering dogs' is overly emotive.
- The final sentence sets up a number of interesting arguments that will presumably be dealt with in later paragraphs.

LESSON 17: RADIO TALK

Learning aim: To write an effective radio talk

- Writing a radio talk is 'writing for the ear'.
- It is important to address the audience directly, using accessible language.
- The language should help the listeners to 'visualise' what they hear.
- News reports for radio should be clear, correct and concise.
- Adopt an appropriate tone – formal for serious news, discussions or voiceovers; less formal for chat shows sports commentary or music programmes.

Read the following two news reports (newspaper and radio), and examine their contrasting styles.

REPORT 1

SPORTS CALL

NEW TALENT BADLY NEEDED!

Mike McCourt reports from Breffni Park.

If this was a dress rehearsal for the championship meeting coming up on May 29, then Sligo boss Ciaran Dennehy may want to audition for some new talent.

His leading men were played off the stage by a Cavan side whose fortunes have undergone an astonishing transformation in the space of seven days. A week earlier in Páirc Tailteann, Cavan – coming off two losses – trailed by 1–6 to 0–2 at half-time against Meath. They looked set for relegation. But they were re-born in the second half to pick up a first win. They certainly continued that form here.

Sligo scorched the earth with powerful running early on. They raced into a three-point lead after five minutes with top-notch scores from Ger O'Hanlon, Seamus Shevlin and Johnny Murtagh. However, the Blues quickly extinguished Sligo's fire. Cavan looked to break out of defence at pace at every opportunity. They reeled off 1–8 without reply before Sligo finally raised another white flag approaching the half hour mark.

Dan Gibney dominated aerial exchanges on the edge of the square. Prodigal son Seanie Thornton was electrifying in their dual attacks. The duo combined to allow Paul Johnston to bundle home an untidy gaol in the seventeenth minute. Points from Dara Sweeney, Johnston and captain Gearoid Lavery and a brace apiece from Mickey Hodgers and corner-back Jason Scully saw them take a commanding lead. Cavan breezed into the break 1–9 to 0–4.

Sub Ethan Richards picked off two hard-won points after the break for Sligo but was soon black-carded. Cavan then tore through at will, with further scores from Thornton and Sweeney. Then Johnston curled a brilliant point before coming off to a rousing reception. With a quarter of an hour left on the clock, the Blues were quietly coasting after Gibney flicked home a second goal. Six minutes later, Man of the Match Thornton sauntered through at ease and side-footed home. That left the final scoreboard reading 3–15 to 0–8. Disappointment for a gallant Sligo side, but a powerful performance from Cavan.

And that's your GAA sport for now on Newsbeat 2FM. Good afternoon.

REPORT 2

- News at One
- This is News at One with Ann Culhane.
- A Garda officer who was injured when his patrol car overturned in Galway on Saturday morning remains in a serious condition in hospital. The 36-year-old Garda was responding to an emergency call when the accident happened shortly after 2.00 a.m. No other vehicle was involved and the relatives of the officer have been informed. The Police Commissioner Nuala O'Halloran has expressed her concern at this latest incident and has visited the officer's family.
- Rescue teams were searching for two mountain climbers on the Carrauntoohil peak in Kerry last night. The couple, from Aberdeen in Scotland, had been climbing in the Hag's Glen region. Local rescue teams have reported that the Devil's Ladder route has become seriously eroded in several places due the heavy rainfall over recent months. The alarm was raised when the climbers failed to turn up at a meeting point. The search has been called off in the last hour due to decreased visibility, but will resume when visibility improves.
- Environmental protestors are blockading one of the main Shell petrol stations in Hudson Bay. They say they're angry at the impact of the oil company's work on the environment and how they treat people in Third World countries. There are now major delays on the N61. Motorists are advised to seek an alternative route.
- That's the news for the moment. Our next report will be at five o'clock this evening. Over to Alan now for the latest weather update.

CLASS/HOMEWORK EXERCISES

Compare the different styles of language used in each of the two news reports above. Refer to at least two features of style in your answer.

Allow about 15–18 minutes for your answer. Aim for at least 150 words.

QUESTION B

Write the text of an entertaining 2FM radio talk that you will present on the subject: 'Song lyrics capture the true spirit of today's younger generation.'

Allow about 35–40 minutes and aim for at least 450 words.

LESSON 18: SHORT SPEECH

Learning aim: To write a short persuasive speech

Comprehending Question B tasks frequently include writing the text of a short speech. A speech is usually more formal than a persuasive talk. The purpose, audience and persona of the writer will all suggest the formal register or tone.

The sample answer on the next page was written in response to the following task:

QUESTION B

Your school's Board of Management has decided not to allow the annual school trip abroad for your Leaving Certificate class. The Student Council disagrees with this decision. As Chairperson of the Student Council, you have been asked to give a short talk to the Board in which you express the students' objection to this decision. You will also put forward a case for the re-instatement of the annual school trip. Write the text of the speech you would make. (50)

Prompt!

Planning is essential to producing a successful response. Study the wording of the question closely and define the task, deciding on the stance or approach.

Ask yourself the following questions:

- **What do I have to write about?** The distress of the students at this cancellation and the reasons for the reversal of this decision.
- **Who am I as the writer?** Chairperson of the Student Council.
- **For whom am I writing?** The Board of Management.
- **Why am I writing this?** To register a complaint and suggest a solution.

  (Stance: Disagree with withdrawal of trip and argue for its reinstatement)
- **What format should be used?** A speech.
- **What type of language will be appropriate?** Formal, rational and reasonable.

Draft Structure

Paragraph 1: Outline – address, introduction, problem, expression of disappointment.

Paragraph 2: Advantage of trip, to learn personal/group responsibility.

Paragraph 3: Another benefit, to acquire negotiation skills.

Paragraph 4: Third advantage, to develop a broad outlook by sampling another culture.

Paragraph 5: Conclusion.

Sample Question B Speech

1. Chairperson of the Board, members of the Board, Principal, I am here today in my capacity as Chairperson of the School Student Council to express the students' great disappointment and dismay at the cancellation of the Sixth Year annual school trip to Italy. I also ask you to reconsider your decision. The Student Council and I appreciate that in this time of recession and with the harsh race for college points, the benefit of school trips has been put under the microscope.' However, valuable life skills are acquired: personal responsibility, group responsibility and a broadening of perspectives.

2. Individual students learn the importance of punctuality and their duty to the group when they must operate to the schedule of the trip. A student learns very quickly the consequences of selfish actions, such as not getting up on time and keeping others waiting. Angry peer faces get results! This is a much more effective way of emphasising the importance of good time-keeping, invaluable to future employers. Personal responsibility is developed through the practicalities of being responsible for one's own passport, money and belongings.

3. Diplomacy and tact are effectively honed through the negotiations of who will share a room with whom. Students learn to compromise and live with someone, other than close family members. Our views on others begin to broaden as we see others, both pupils and teachers, in a new and different light in these unfamiliar surroundings. The cosy, familiar group of friends is now no longer there and we must mix with other students with whom we may not have associated before because they were in different classes or had different interests. This will be our last opportunity to reach out because next year we will all be scattered into our various chosen fields of study or work.

4. Nothing can compare to seeing and experiencing the treasures of a European city in reality. No virtual tour can capture the beauty and majesty of Michelangelo's statue of David in Florence or the exquisite skin tones of the famous Botticelli painting, 'Birth of Venus'. Over the years, countless students have been introduced to great works of art on our annual cultural tours abroad – and it's important that this important tradition is continued.

5. Therefore, I urge you, on behalf of the very disappointed Sixth year students, to revisit your decision to cancel this year's trip to Italy. Education is more than a frenzied scurry for points; it is the development of the individual student's potential for living life to the best of one's ability and making an effective contribution to society. This year marks the end of our secondary school phase – so, what better way to round off our time here than by experiencing the school trip of a lifetime.

6. There is no substitute for real experience in the wider world. Travel really does broaden the mind. We learn to recognise our duties to ourselves, our group and to expand our viewpoints on people and places. Thank you for giving me the opportunity to express the students' views on this matter and we look forward to hearing your decision.

Examiner's comment

- A focused and informative response.
- Arguments are structured logically – three distinct advantages of school outings are clearly developed.
- Language is persuasive throughout. Key verbs ('ask', 'urge') appeal directly to the Management Board.
- Paragraphs 2 and 3 include compelling reasons for retention of school trips.
- Repetition of the word 'important' in paragraph 4 should have been avoided.
- The colourful illustrations in paragraph 4 are particularly convincing. Overall, the serious formal tone works well, building to a strong ending that rounds off the speech effectively. (48/50)

GRADE: H1

P = 15/15

C = 14/15

L = 14/15

M = 5/5

TOTAL = 48/50

THE RULE OF THREE

A powerful speech writing technique is the **Rule of Three** (or **power of three**). This writing principle suggests that information that comes in threes is most likely to be remembered. This is because having three entities combines both brevity and rhythm with having the smallest amount of information to create a catchy pattern.

Speakers often use three adjectives or phrases to emphasise a point, for example:

Homework is dull, time-consuming and uninteresting.

That's the truth, the whole truth and nothing but the truth.

Some famous **Rule of Three** speech examples include:

Julius Caesar (Roman emperor):

Veni, vidi, vici (I came, I saw, I conquered)

Abraham Lincoln (American president):

Government of the people, by the people, for the people

French motto:

Liberté, égalité, fraternité (Liberty, equality, fraternity)

Comprehending B

Quick practice

1. The following extract is taken from a political speech. Identify and write out two sentences from it that use the Rule of Three.

My fellow citizens,

I stand here today humbled by the task before us, grateful for the trust you have bestowed, mindful of the sacrifices borne by our ancestors. I thank President Bush for the generosity and cooperation he has shown throughout the transition. That we are in the midst of a crisis is well understood. Our nation is at war, against a far-reaching network of violence and hatred. Our economy is badly weakened, a consequence of greed and irresponsibility on the part of some, but also our collective failure to make hard choices and prepare the nation for a new age. Homes have been lost; jobs shed; businesses shuttered.

2. Choose the correct word or phrase from the following list to finish these examples of the Rule of Three.

play, listen, roll, stronger, mineral, go, got the t-shirt, brighter, speak no evil, money

(a) Hear no evil, see no evil,...

(b) Stop, look,...

(c) Work, rest,...

(d) Animal, vegetable,...

(e) Faster, higher,...

(f) Time, effort,...

(g) Shake, rattle,...

(h) Ready, steady,...

(i) Seen it, done it,...

(j) Bigger, better,...

SUCCESSFUL ANSWERING

How do I organise my speech and write a good concluding paragraph?

Another use of the Rule of Three is to help shape your speech so that it is easy for your audience to grasp your argument.

1. Introduction: tell your listeners what you are going to say.

2. Main body: say it.

3. Conclusion: tell them what you said (repetition is another powerful speech writing technique).

CLASS/HOMEWORK EXERCISE

QUESTION B

The school has decided to close the school library and turn it into a computer room. Write the text of a speech you would make to the Parents' Council, as Chairperson of the Student Council, expressing the dismay of the student body and making a case to retain the library. (50)

Allow 35–40 minutes and aim for at least 450 words.

Prompt!

- Before you start, make out headings for a five-paragraph plan. (Keep in mind the content, persona, audience, purpose, register and genre.) Points might include the lack of suitable teen literature at home, the delights of discovering a new author by browsing the book shelves, acquiring the habit of solo reading and learning, prominence of technological devices in students' lives already, or the availability of other locations for a computer room, etc.
- To put forward a successful argument, the speaker has to make a rational, logical case to the audience, rather than appealing only to emotion or recounting personal anecdotes.

TECHNIQUES OF ARGUMENTATIVE WRITING INCLUDE:

- Gaining the audience's attention from the start by outlining the argument
- Using a clear, structured argument to convince the audience through logic
- Making use of rhetorical devices, such as repetition and the Rule of Three
- Assuming a formal, measured tone

Your careers will be determined largely by how well you speak, by how well you write and by the quality of your ideas… in that order.

Patrick Henry Winston

LESSON 19: DIARY WRITING

Learning aim: To write an effective diary entry

Before the age of social media and blogs, the best way to record your life was through a written diary or journal. A diary is an account of personal experiences. It can also record thoughts, feelings and reflections.

Diaries can be interesting documents that reveal a story of a certain event, time or place.

Entries are usually chronological and have a sense of sequence, with specific dates or times given before each entry.

The language is often note-like and the tone is usually chatty, informal and confessional. Diary entries should always be written in the first person and include specific dates or times.

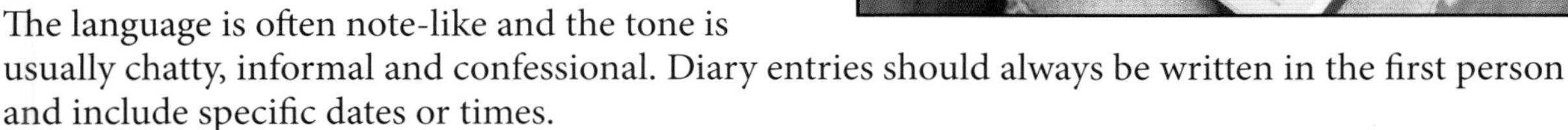

Prompt!

Comprehending B questions often include diary writing tasks. These are sometimes based directly on one of the three comprehending texts.

You may be asked to assume the personality of a character from the text.

When writing diary entries give careful consideration to your language style, which should achieve a sense of the character's point of view and 'voice'.

Sample Diary

Dr Clare O'Leary gives her amazing account of how she cheated death to become the first Irishwoman to conquer Mount Everest.

April 17

As we started out, I noticed there were only Sherpas on the route – no foreigners – and this worried me too; had we made a wrong decision?

As we continued upwards, the weather began to clear, the winds stopped and the sun rose. I started to relax and enjoy things more. After five hours, we reached Camp 1. My legs had stopped working; I was tired thirsty and hungry. I didn't know how I was going to keep climbing for another four hours. Pat passed me some hot juice for energy.

Soon we were on the move again. I hated being the slowest. When we reached Camp 2, I was wrecked and had a bad headache. I went to bed almost immediately although it was only 3.00 pm.

May 5

'Hurry up Clare, it's 6.45 am.' I was jolted out of my sleep. 'What's up?' I asked, wondering for a minute where I was. 'The winds have settled a little and we're going to go for it; we leave in 15 minutes.'

We started to move at 7.10 a.m. We walked for over two hours across the glacier. As I gazed up the steep Lohtse face, I could see tiny figures like ants balancing on it. A wave of terror passed over me and I wondered if I was really up for this. I used my jumar exactly as I had learnt. If I slipped, I knew I would fall a long, long way.
It was a long 6–7 hours before we reached our tent, where I managed to drink a little black tea and then fell asleep – utterly exhausted.

May 12–13

Pat got a weather forecast text message sent to his phone and it looks like the weather high on the mountain is going to be good for climbing in the next few days. I took my Irish flag out of my suitcase and packed it carefully into the bottom of my rucksack; as I did so, I was thinking of what it would be like when we reached the summit and how proud I'd be to wave the tricolour and claim to be the first Irishwoman to reach the summit of Mount Everest!

May 18

On top of the world (29, 035ft). I made it! I made it to the summit of Mount Everest! At 6.45 this morning, Pat, Pemba, Lhakpa, Nang Chemmi, Jangbu, Lamababu and I took our final steps onto the top of the world. I've never felt as happy in my whole life!
The view was amazing as the whole world lay under our feet. After taking loads of pictures and calling Base Camp and our families back home, we started to make our way back down to the South Col, where I am resting at the moment. I'm so exhausted all I want to do is sleep!

Comprehending B

CLASS/HOMEWORK EXERCISES

1. **Outline, in your own words, any three observations made by Clare O'Leary in her diary. Support your answer with reference to the text.**
2. **Briefly describe the type of language used by the writer? Give two examples to illustrate your answer.**

QUESTION B

Write at least three diary entries that record the details of a disastrous holiday (real or imaginary) that you experienced in a foreign country. (50)

Allow about 35–40 minutes and aim for at least 450 words.

Sample answer 1

22nd July

Dear Diary
I've been here a week now but it feels as though I've been here a year. I'm counting down the days until I get home – fourteen to be exact. There are six people in the

family with whom my uncle does business. They are polite to me, but make me feel like such an inconvenience. I thought that I would be minding children, but all four children are older than me. The father, Pierre, is away a lot and the mother Marie-Claire drinks alcohol like water and yesterday I was in the car with her and I was afraid that we would crash. Mum rang the house last night, but I heard Marie-Claire saying that I was gone swimming with Sophie, their youngest daughter. She had hung up by the time I reached the phone. I really want to talk to my Mum and Dad, but I can't complain, they have spent good money on my air fare and I can't come home early. Keep positive – only two weeks left!!

1st August

Dear Diary,

Going home in four days I have only talked to Mum once since I came here and that was when I answered the phone myself. I didn't tell her how unhappy I was, I didn't want to worry her. Each day here is so long and I've nothing to do! I sit in the garden all day while Sophie and her two older sisters and brother go the beach and go shopping. I've no transport to any of these places. I am becoming increasingly more paranoid that they are laughing at me. I haven't learnt anything since arriving here as no one talks to me to help me practise my French. I know I only have four days left but I hope they pass quickly because I really want to go home!

5th August

Dear Diary,

At last I am sitting on the Aer Lingus plane, breathing a huge sigh of relief. Marie-Claire drove at breakneck speed this morning and dumped me and my suitcase at the airport, turned on her heel and went in search of 'refreshments'! That was the last I saw of her. My flight was called and here I am. It's definitely 'Adieu' to France and the family and holiday from hell.

GRADE: H3

P = 11/15

C = 10/15

L = 9/15

M = 5/5

TOTAL = 35/50

Examiner's comment

- Good detailed opening section provides informative background.
- This could have been developed more to give a sense of French culture.
- Further details (about places, food, etc.) would have added interest.
- Accurate mechanics, apt tone and language control throughout.
- Slightly short and repetitive. (34/50)

Comprehending B

QUESTION B

Write three or more diary entries that record your experiences when taking part in a talent show. Explain what took place beforehand, the performance itself and what happened afterwards. (50)

Allow about 35–40 minutes and aim for at least 450 words.

Sample answer 2

28th February

Dear Diary,
All my dreams have come true! On RTÉ tonight an advert appeared for an Irish talent show, 'Star Talent 2'. I quickly scribbled down the details – audition in a few weeks' time, final to be televised, all acts welcome. Immediately, I texted Jane and Emma. I was going to form Ireland's best ever singing and dancing girl band, a true rival to Little Mix and The Pussycat Dolls. This was truly monumental! We are going to meet tomorrow evening in the gym for our rehearsal.

1st March

Dear Diary,
What a complete disaster! The girls arrived and the gym was locked. After wandering around in the rain (bad hair day!) we eventually located Mr Doyle and he agreed to open the gym for us. Further problems! Nobody could agree on the name for the group. I thought my name should go first, as after all, I was the one who saw the advert, came up with the idea of a group and organised the rehearsing schedule. 'Tina and the Turnips' had quite a nice ring to it. However, Emma cut up rough. She said she didn't want to be known as a turnip head, and Jane agreed. I was out-voted. So 'The Teensters' it is. I think it's a bit 'Glee', don't you?

3rd March

Dear Diary,
Rehearsal 2 and we tried to agree on a song. Well, you would think War of the Worlds had erupted. Jane's shrill tones pierced the air like flying missiles as she screamed 'Don't Stop Believing' over and over again. Emma agreed with Jane and yes, you've guessed it I was out-voted again. But I am thankful that my eardrums are still in working order! That ended our first 'rehearsal'. We didn't sing. We didn't dance. But wow! Could we argue!

17th March

Dear Diary,
I have not written to you for a long time as every bone in my body is so tired. We've been selected for the final. We have rehearsed and rehearsed. I can carry all the notes and the girls' dance routine is sharp and edgy. We had one last tremendous fight about what we were going to wear and personally I think we look like foil-wrapped chickens, but I didn't argue much as I look like the leader of the group! We were quite nervous tonight during the dress rehearsal, but it went well as even Mr Doyle emerged from the shadows and clapped.

Comprehending B

20th March

Dear Diary,
The day of the final arrives and it's all over in a flash. We stood in a long queue with metal barriers dividing us into lines as we awaited the grand entrance of the judges. I could feel the cold sweat running down my neck as we stood waiting. Emma and Jane were very pale and I was as red as a tomato. Suddenly we were on. The music blared, the lights flashed and finally my big moment had arrived. My voice soared and I 'believed' as waves of wild applause washed over us. The judges were on their feet. It was brilliant! This was what was meant to be.

Examiner's comment

- A very good series of focused diary entries.
- Details provide interest throughout.
- Tone is scintillating, engaging and humorous.
- Appropriate expression throughout and a good sense of sequence.
- Sparkling writing, entertaining and well-sustained narrative voice. (48/50)

GRADE: H1

P = 15/15

C = 14/15

L = 14/15

M = 5/5

TOTAL = 48/50

CLASS/HOMEWORK EXERCISE

QUESTION B

Write at least three diary entries that record your experiences when taking part in either a musical, dramatic or sports competition in your school.

Describe what happened beforehand, the event itself and the aftermath. (50)

Allow about 35–40 minutes and aim for at least 450 words.

Writing in a diary is a really strange experience for someone like me. Not only because I've never written anything before, but also because it seems to me that later on neither I nor anyone else will be interested in the musings of a thirteen-year-old school girl. Oh well, it doesn't matter. I feel like writing.

Anne Frank

I never travel without my diary. One should always have something sensational to read in the train.

Oscar Wilde

LESSON 20: INTERVIEWS

Learning aim: To write the text of an effective interview

- Interviews vary from face-to-face meetings to Skype, telephone and email exchanges.
- Typical examples relate to jobs and careers, research, celebrity interviews, etc.
- The interviewer decides the purpose of the interview and the audience for which it is intended.
- Questions should be short and open-ended to allow the interviewee to give apt responses (clear factual information and/or anecdotes).
- Avoid closed Yes/No questions.
- Answers should give a sense of the interviewee through the expression of personal opinions, the description of first-hand experiences and the recollection of emotional or significant events.
- The tone should be open and sincere, but can be both formal and informal. Avoid using jargon.
- When appropriate, aim for a lively journalistic style focused on keeping the reader involved and interested.

Sample Interview

Lauren Laverne meets author JK Rowling

JK Rowling, author of numerous successful books, including the Harry Potter series.

Lauren Laverne, radio and TV broadcaster, and former lead singer of Kenickie.

LL OK, let's chat. So apparently this is part of a series about how the art of conversation is dying. And I'm not sure if we're a test case or...

JR Let's prove them wrong!

LL But I thought I'd ask what kind of conversations you like the best – who do you like to talk to the most?

JR Well, it's very corny, but my husband is definitely my best friend. My sister. I'm a small-group person. My dream is a small group I know very well, then we have an intense conversation. I don't want an argument, but I want a conversation about things that really matter.

LL I wanted to ask you about naming things, because you have an interesting relationship with the power of names. Obviously, having written under different pseudonyms, and having characters with these wonderful, Dickensian, perfectly fitting names.

JR I think they were offering odds of 100–1 that I'd call my son Voldemort. 100–1! It was worth a bet. But you're right, names are really important. Choosing a pseudonym for Robert Galbraith was a really big deal.

LL But didn't you have 12 rejections for Harry Potter?

JR Do you know, I read all sorts of numbers and I don't actually know. But a good few, yes.

LL And were they more wounding? What kept you going?

JR [Long pause] That's such a good question because you know I was not confident then at all. But I wanted it so badly, I wasn't going to give up. And I don't think I've ever felt, before or since, anything like the elation of realising I was going to be published.

LL How did you find out?

JR My agent rang me and… he was so low key about it! One publisher had kept it for six months, which obviously gave me a lot of hope, and then they said no. I was devastated. Then [my agent] phoned me up and said, 'Well, Bloomsbury want it' – very casual! Not realising he's giving me the gift of my life. And there was this long pause, and I just said: 'So… you're saying I am going to be published?' I was beside myself.

LL Terrible Pete Best moment for whoever passed on it.

JR You know, I can say this now, I was quite diffident about saying it for a long time. But I did have a belief, with Harry, that the difficult thing would be persuading someone to take it, because it didn't fit. People said children's books had to be half the length, and what an old-fashioned subject, a boarding school. I did have this feeling that the difficult thing would be persuading someone to publish it – but that if it was, people would like it.

LL I wondered how you measured success. I read your Wikipedia because we were doing this…

JR Oh God, have you read it? I've never read it. I've read yours.

LL You've done quite well, Jo.

JR Cheers, Lauren.

LL But once you've got the Légion d'honneur, how do you measure it?

JR It's really weird you're asking me that question, because four days ago I wrote the answer in the fourth Robert Galbraith book. Because when you meet my detective in book four, he is reflecting on how success never feels the way you think it will be. Some people would assume that you're sitting around feeling simply marvellous and shining your baubles. But I remember, a week after I got my American deal, which got me a lot of press, one of my very best girlfriends rang me and said, 'I thought you'd sound so elated.' From the outside, I'm sure everything looked amazing. But in my flat, where I was still a single mum and I didn't know who to call to do my hair, everything felt phenomenally overwhelming. For the first time in my life I could buy a house, which meant security for my daughter and me, but I now felt: 'The next book can't possibly live up to this.' So I managed to turn this amazing triumph into tragedy, in the space of about five days.

LL Yeah: now do it again! But the Harry Potter legend is it came to you as a kind of universe, in its entirety.

JR There is truth to that. It was like an explosion of colour, and I could see lots of detail about the world. Of course the whole seven-book plot didn't come at once, but the basic premises were there.

LL I wondered whether you might like radio.

JR I love radio.

LL But you'd be great on the radio!

JR Well, it's my favourite medium.

JR I do see you as far cooler than me.

LL Are you kidding me?

JR You definitely are. And that was fun.

LL That was really fun.

Word Power

There are two basic types of interview questions – Yes/No questions and 'Wh'- questions.

* **Yes/No questions** are called closed questions because there are only two possible answers.

* **Wh- questions** allow the respondent to expand on the answer. These questions begin with who, what, where, why, when (and how).

The text above shows some of the important aspects of good interviewing. Lauren Laverne uses **open questions** in her interview to allow JK Rowling to make fuller responses: 'But I thought I'd ask what kind of conversations you like the best – who do you like to talk to most?

This gives the interviewee an opportunity to explain that she likes to talk to her family about things that really matter.

Note that Rowling uses **personal anecdotes** in her answers, e.g. 'I remember, a week after I got my American deal, which got me a lot of press, one of my very best girlfriends rang me…'

This allows the reader to gain an **insight into her personality** and the interview becomes engaging.

The interview ends on a courteous note – 'That was really fun'.

CLASS/HOMEWORK EXERCISE

1. Imagine that you are interviewing JK Rowling. Arrange the following questions into two separate lists of Yes/No questions and Wh- questions

(a) Have you written many books?

(b) Are you working on one at the moment?

(c) Who is your publisher?

(d) Has your publisher ever let you down?

(e) What did they say to your success?

(f) When is your next book due?

(g) Can you write in the morning?

(h) How did you come up with the plot for your latest book?

(i) Which is your favourite 'Harry Potter' book?

(j) Do you have a plan before you start to write?

CLASS/HOMEWORK EXERCISE

QUESTION B

Write the text of an interview (questions and answers) which you carried out with a famous person who was a past pupil of your school and achieved success in the world of politics, celebrity or sport. This interview will be published in your next school magazine. (50)

Allow about 35–40 minutes and aim for at least 450 words.

Prompt!

- Try to avoid lengthy or clichéd interview questions.
- Instead of 'Did you like school?', consider 'What is your outstanding memory of your schooldays?'
- Avoid general questions: 'How did you achieve your sporting success?' 'What are your hobbies?'
- Good interview questions are unbiased (neutral) and allow the interviewee to express his or her own response.
- Boring questions lead to boring answers. Use lively approaches. For example, you could ask 'They call you the Superman of sport... what three qualities do you think you share with Superman?'
- Pick the most provocative questions and answers – these should be featured at the beginning and at the end.

> The person telling the story is the expert when it comes to his or her life, and he or she may tell unexpected things in unexpected ways.
>
> J. Eyles and E. Perry

LESSON 22: INFORMAL LETTERS

Learning aim: To write an effective informal letter

Personal letters were once a common part of life. It could be argued that digital forms of communicating such as email, SMS, Snapchat and Skype, etc. have made this mode of communication out-of-date. However, letters add a uniquely personal touch, usually requiring the writer to think more about the main idea, details or an introduction rather than firing off a quick note. Informal personal letters are mostly written to friends or family. These letters share thoughts, feelings and experiences. They contain an element of reflection often missing from electronic messaging.

CLASS/HOMEWORK EXERCISE

Read the letter below from the American writer, Maya Angelou, dedicated to the daughter she never had and identify *two* of the reflections she shares with her 'daughter'. Give your reasons why they would (or would not) be as successful if communicated electronically.

Dear Marguerite,

You're itching to be on your own. You don't want anybody telling you what time you have to be in at night or how to raise your baby. You're going to leave your mother's big comfortable house and she won't stop you, because she knows you too well.

But listen to what she says:

When you walk out of my door, don't let anybody raise you – you've been raised.

You know right from wrong. In every relationship you make, you'll have to show readiness to adjust and make adaptations.

Remember, you can always come home.

You will go home again when the world knocks you down or – when you fall down in full view of the world. But only for two or three weeks at a time. Your mother will pamper you and feed you your favorite meal of red beans and rice. You'll make a practice of going home so she can liberate you again – one of the greatest gifts along with nurturing your courage, that she will give you.

Be courageous, but not foolhardy.

Walk proud as you are,

Maya

Prompt!

- Letters to friends and family should have your address at the top right-hand corner and should include the date beneath the address.
- Start the letter with 'Dear Kate' or 'Hi John' or some other friendly greeting.
- Your closing should be equally friendly and informal, e.g. 'Love', 'See you soon', 'Best wishes' and will be accompanied by your first name.
- The language should be lively, chatty and informal.
- In the exam, you may be asked to adopt a persona [take on the role of another person] and speak in that character's voice, e.g. you may be asked to write a letter as a parent to a child. In this case, you must express your letter in an adult voice and give an adult's point of view.
- The letter should have an introduction, body [main section] and ending.
- Grammar and spelling are important for clear communication. Contractions [e.g. 'I'm' instead of 'I am'] and less formal punctuation [dashes, exclamation marks, etc.] are acceptable.

QUESTION B

Write a letter to your imaginary future son or daughter offering him or her advice about coping with the pressures of adolescence. [50]

Allow about 35–40 minutes and aim for at least 450 words.

Sample Answer: Informal letter

15, Gresham Street
Cork
6th March

Dear Saoirse,

You probably won't want to listen to advice from me, after all no teen likes their mother or father telling them what to do. What would we know? The world has changed from when we were teenagers long, long ago. That's just what I thought when I was your age so I just tuned out when adults started to lecture me. I'm not going to lecture. I'm just going to tell you what I have found out.

Exams! You stress too much about points and exam results. Doing the best you can do is enough. There is no need to try to be the best. Be the best you can be. There is no need to be perfect. Perfection doesn't exist in this imperfect world. How boring if everyone was the same and did the same things. Life is great because of its variety. You are you, unique and special.

Friends! It hurts when friends move on without you. During the teenage years, people grow at different rates and change and drift apart. It doesn't mean there is anything wrong with you. It doesn't mean you are being rejected. It is just the ebb and flow of life. Recognising and accepting change is part (a difficult part) of growing up. When you go to college or work you will be meeting new people and making new friends and then you will see that change can also be a good thing and a very important part of life.

Decisions! You feel overwhelmed with career choices, CAO and UCAS forms, deadlines. There are also decisions to be made in your personal life. Take one thing at a time. In your career path decisions can be changed. In your personal life, be true to yourself. Trust your gut instinct and if you feel uncomfortable, don't do it. You have to follow your own instincts, which can be scary but exhilarating. Be confident. Be strong. Do your own thing. Respect others.

Read – the writers have seen and done it all!

I've tried not to lecture, but I probably have. I will always worry about you. That's my job. You are on your own, but you are well able for it. I trust you to do the right thing.

Good luck,

Dad

Checklist

- [ ] Is the letter addressed properly? Is it dated?
- [ ] Is the sign-off correct for an informal letter?
- [ ] Is it well laid out/planned?
- [ ] Is the tone chatty and informal?

CLASS/HOMEWORK EXERCISE

Read the following two letters and list *three similarities* between them. In your answer, consider some of the following: address, date, opening greeting, signing off, tone and content.

Letter 1: Excerpt from a 19th-century informal personal letter written by the novelist Jane Austen to her sister Cassandra.

Godmersham Park
August 24, 1805

My dear Cassandra,

How do you do; and how is Harriot's cold? I hope at this time you are sitting down to answer these questions.

Yesterday was a very quiet day with us; my noisiest efforts were writing to Frank, and playing at battledore and shuttlecock with William; he and I have practised together two mornings, and improve a little; we have fequently kept it up three times, and once or twice six.

I have found your white mittens; they were folded up within my clean nightcap, and send their duty to you.

Mr Hall walked off this morning to Ospringe, with no inconsiderable booty. He charged Elizabeth five shillings for every time of dressing her hair, and five shillings for every lesson to Sace, allowing nothing for the pleasures of his visit here, for meat, drink, and lodging, the benefit of country air, and the charms of Mrs Salked's and Mrs Sace's society. Towards me he was as considerate as I had hoped for fom my relationship with you, charging me only two shillings and sixpence for cutting my hair, though it was as thoroughly dressed after being cut for Eastwell as it had been for the Ashford assembly. He certainly respects either our youth or our poverty.

Give my best love to Harriot, and kind remembrance to her brothers,

Yours very affectionately,

J. A.

Letter 2: A modern-day informal personal letter between two old school friends, one of whom has emigrated.

'Ghan House'
Beresford Road
Co. Dublin
13th May

Dear Séan,

Hope you had a great New Year! How are things in the land of the maple leaf? Gosh, I really envy you getting that position in Ottawa! I'm stuck here in the Emerald Isle, except it looks more like a still from Game of Thrones, Hibernia. Brrr! I heard that the pay and conditions are really good there.

Did you hear about Madge Johnson? She has just left for Singapore. It was a bit of a shock because she had gone through two years of nursing college. She just up and went. Gone! Nobody's too sure what happened, but there are rumours of a personal meltdown. She took it hard when Joe went off with Charlene. I'll keep you posted if I hear more. I know you'll want to know!!

I'm quite busy myself. Just joined the lads in Google, room for advancement there! I am enjoying it so far. Whether I'll feel the same in two years' time, I don't know. Perhaps I'll join you in Canada!

We are still playing footie and are managing to get two or three practices in a week. The other lads were asking for you. Have you joined anything over there? Are you sliding about with an ice-hockey stick? Let me know. Must go now. The rest of the gang are about to call round to go to Vicar Street. Hozier is playing tonight.

Keep me posted whenever you can. I enjoy keeping in touch and receiving details of your adventures in Canada.

Cheers!

Daniel

CLASS/HOMEWORK EXERCISE

QUESTION B

Imagine yourself fifteen years from now. You have achieved great success and public recognition in your chosen career. Write a letter from your 'older self' to you at your present age about the influences and experiences that helped you on the path to success. (50)

Allow about 35–40 minutes and aim for at least 450 words.

Prompt!

- **What do I have to write about?** The influences and experiences that helped me to succeed in my chosen career.
- **Who am I as the writer?** My adult self.
- **To whom am I writing?** My present self.
- **Why am I writing this?** To inspire and encourage myself to be the best I can be.
- **What format should be used?** An informal letter.
- **What type of language will be appropriate?** Informal, chatty, friendly and encouraging.

Draft Structure

Paragraph 1: Introduction – where I am now as an adult.

Paragraph 2: Where I was as a teenager.

Paragraph 3: Influences/experiences that helped me succeed.

Paragraph 4: Obstacles overcome.

Paragraph 5: Conclusion.

The ready communication through electronic means that has replaced the hand-written note is wonderful. But we have definitely lost something here, and those Skype, email and text exchanges won't be treasured in the way that my teenage letters, scribbled journals and postcards have been for years.

Philip Hensher (Wall Street Journal)

LESSON 23: MEMOS

Learning aim: To write an effective business memo

The term 'memo' is short for 'memorandum' – something to be remembered. It is mainly used as a formal business communication to bring attention to problems and a solution to problems. Memos inform the recipient about new information, such as policy changes, price increases, briefings, proposals, etc. They often persuade the recipient to take an action, e.g. attend a meeting or implement a new production procedure.

* A memo is usually not as formal as a written letter.
* The tone is generally friendly as it is a communication between colleagues.
* Memos should be concise and to the point.
* If necessary, a memo may begin with a brief introductory paragraph to introduce the reason for the memo.
* Memos often use bullet points to explain the most important information.
* A courteous 'thank you' to round off is sufficient to conclude the memo.

Sample Memo

QUESTION B

Write a memo to customers about the availability of nutritional facts in a firm's products.

MEMORANDUM

To: All customers of Cherry's Cupcakes

From: H. R. Johnson, Customer Relations

Date: 29th January

Subject: Publication of Nutrition Facts

Due to extensive customer feedback, we at Cherry's Cupcakes would like to demonstrate our commitment to making healthy choices by publishing detailed nutritional information for all our baked goods. Although our stores are not by law required to provide the nutritional facts of our products, we agree that customers should have access to as much information as possible before making a purchase.

We are confident that you, the customer, will feel better in choosing our cupcakes now that you are aware of these facts. Cherry's Cupcakes are committed to using superior locally grown ingredients in our baked goods. We have gluten-free and vegan options. All our products are prepared and baked in our premises each morning. We also cater for special occasions with treats which are still healthy so the customer can indulge, yet not feel guilty.

All of our nutritional information will be available online, along with a list of ingredients and possible substitutions for those with special dietary requirements. In-store colour pamphlets with the same information will be provided free-of-charge.

We, at Cherry's Cupcakes, value our customers and are delighted that you not only enjoy our products, but make the best healthy choices for you and your family.

Best wishes,
Henry Johnson

Word Power

Close analysis of the structure used in this sample provides a greater understanding of how to write effective memos.

Study the organisation of the information in the sample memo:

(a) Heading
To: Full names and job titles, if appropriate
From: Your name and job title
Date: Current date
Subject: What the memo is about

(b) Opening
Gives the purpose of the memo, the context and the specific assignment or task. It gives a brief overview of what the memo is about. Keep the subject line specific and concise.

(c) Context
Explains the background of the problem you are solving.

(d) Task
What you are doing to help solve the problem.

(e) Discussion
Includes the supporting ideas and research that back up your argument in the memo. Include strong points and evidence to persuade the reader to follow your recommended actions.

(f) Closing
Contains a courteous ending that states what action you require the recipient to take.

CLASS/HOMEWORK EXERCISE

QUESTION B

Imagine that you work as a Research Assistant at Spring Clothes Promotions. Write a memo to the Head of Marketing suggesting changes in the company's advertising that would increase sales. (50)

Allow about 35–40 minutes and aim for at least 450 words.

Prompt!

Use the **sample memo structure** above to guide you. Remember that this memo should persuade.

- **Heading:** As in sample.
- **Opening:** Market research shows that the proposed advertising for the new spring lines need to be re-prioritised and changed. Findings from focus groups and surveys suggest that we need to update our advertising efforts to appeal to the youth market... (complete the paragraph).
- **Context:** Television advertising. In the past, the firm placed adverts during the commercial breaks in shows like Home and Away, but even the face of television is changing and young teens no longer watch these shows... (complete the paragraph).
- **Discussion:** Internet advertising. Spring Clothes need to focus advertising on internet lifestyle sites that appeal to young people... (complete the paragraph).
- **Closing:** As in sample.

  I will be glad to discuss this recommendation with you during our weekly Monday breakfast meeting and follow through any suggestions you make. (Round off).

LESSON 24: PROPOSALS

Learning aim: To write an effective proposal

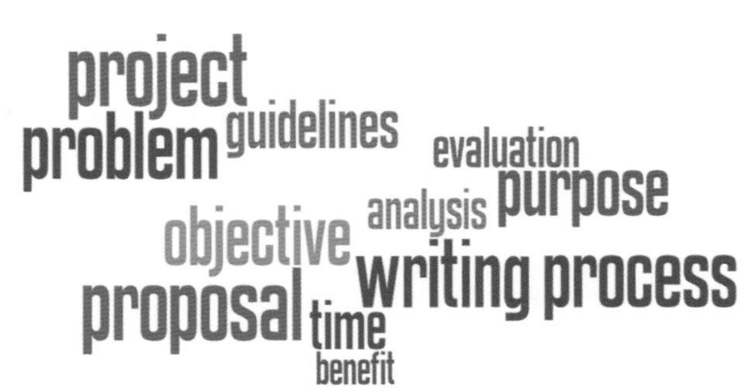

- Proposals are usually action plans for the future. They are very similar to reports, but are aimed at persuading and making recommendations.
- When writing a proposal, it is essential to identify your audience and to explain your ideas or suggestions, providing whatever background is appropriate.
- Write in an accessible straightforward style – clear, correct and concise. Your argument can be persuasive, but must rely on hard facts to be convincing.
- Adopt an appropriate formal tone, avoiding slang, colloquialisms, jargon and clichés.
- The proposal should be positive, logical and practical. It should also include a timeline and details about cost.
- The conclusion should mirror the introduction, emphasising the benefits of your proposal.
- Thank the audience for their time and consideration of the proposal.

Sample Proposal

QUESTION B

Write a short email to your School Student Council Chairperson attaching a proposal to be submitted to the School Board of Management. The proposal (in attachment form) asks the school management to consider supplying new blinds for the Sixth Year classrooms.

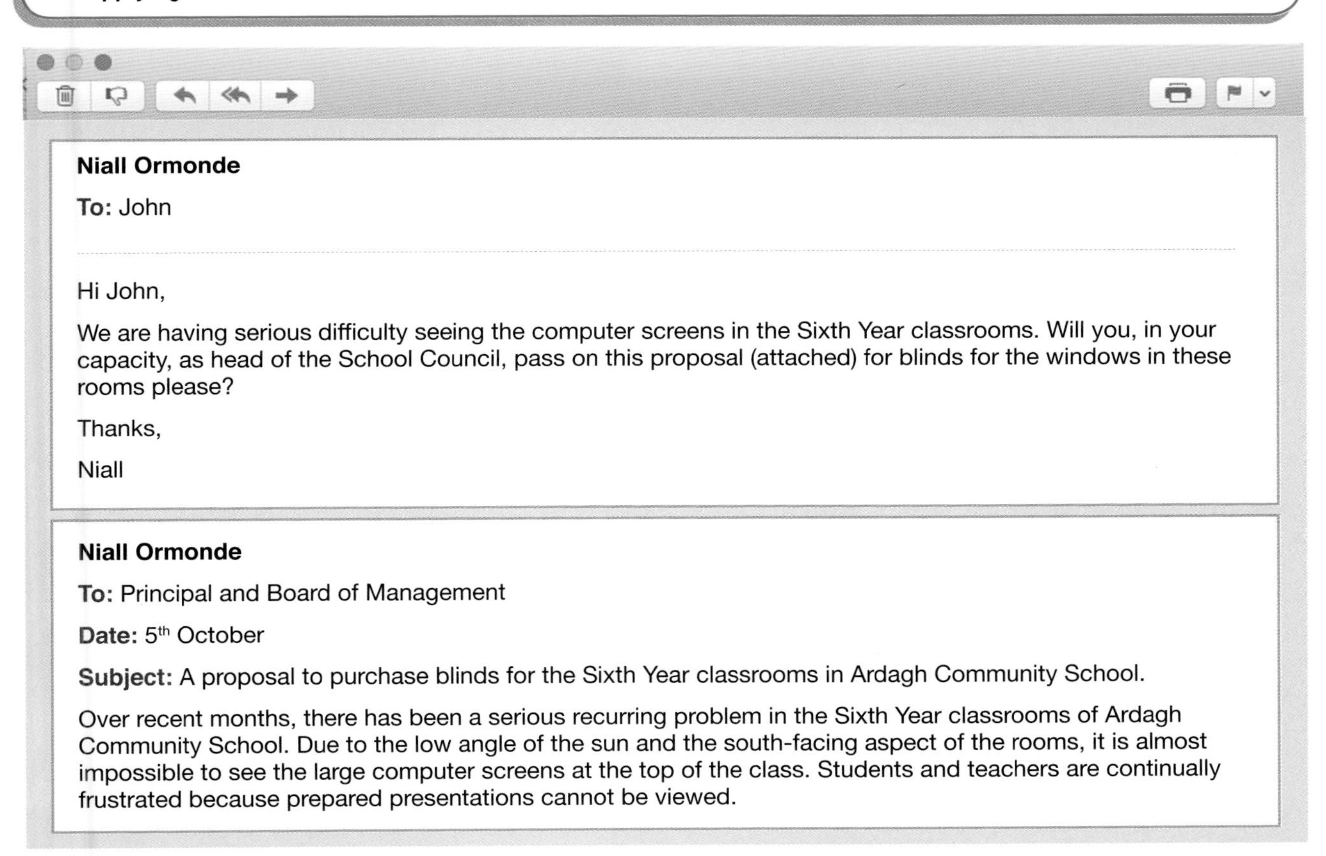

Niall Ormonde

To: John

Hi John,

We are having serious difficulty seeing the computer screens in the Sixth Year classrooms. Will you, in your capacity, as head of the School Council, pass on this proposal (attached) for blinds for the windows in these rooms please?

Thanks,

Niall

Niall Ormonde

To: Principal and Board of Management

Date: 5th October

Subject: A proposal to purchase blinds for the Sixth Year classrooms in Ardagh Community School.

Over recent months, there has been a serious recurring problem in the Sixth Year classrooms of Ardagh Community School. Due to the low angle of the sun and the south-facing aspect of the rooms, it is almost impossible to see the large computer screens at the top of the class. Students and teachers are continually frustrated because prepared presentations cannot be viewed.

It is suggested that blinds are installed in the five Sixth Year classrooms as soon as possible so that students and teachers can prepare for this year's Leaving Certificate examination without unnecessary delays and inconvenience.

There are over 120 Sixth Years who occupy the Sixth Year rooms for at least 5/6 periods every school day. None of the classrooms has blinds fitted. Not only is it impossible to see the screens, but students are obliged to re-arrange the furniture because of the intensity of the sun's rays and also to open the windows due to the heat. This adds a further strain to teaching and learning because the open windows allow the continuous sound of traffic outside to enter the room. The inability to access the IT facilities obviously impedes academic progress and hinders engagement in the study of important subjects.

The Board of Management, in collaboration with the School Council, has raised funds to equip these rooms with state-of-the-art computer technology. But these are useless if the students cannot access the screen and have a cool, quiet environment in which to learn. The re-arranging of heavy school furniture also results in extra work for the caretakers because desks and chairs are being damaged due to the constant movement. The wooden floor has also become scuffed and marked. This is resulting in further costs to the running of the school.

It is proposed that three roller blinds for each of the five Sixth Year classrooms are purchased. These will block the glare and filter the excessive heat. Plastic venetian blinds were installed in the past, but became broken very quickly. Roller blinds are a sturdier option.

Magno-Blinds carry several heavy-duty roller blinds. They come in a variety of light colours which will filter out excess light but which will allow sufficient light through so that electric lights will not be required all day. Such blinds are currently in use in St Macartan's College and the School Principal there has informed me that he would have no hesitation in recommending this brand.

Each blind costs only €160 (including installation) from Magno-Blinds. However, this firm will offer a 20% discount if the purchase is for ten blinds or more. As we are members of the Green World Schools programme, we can also apply for their 2% discount because we will be conserving electricity from reduced light usage. These two discounts will make a significant reduction to the overall cost. Several other local suppliers have an initial cheaper price than Magno-Blinds, but there is a fee for installation and no discount.

In conclusion, the purchase of new blinds for the Sixth Year classrooms would be of tremendous benefit to Ardagh Community School. This would put an end to the persistent traffic noise, as well as reducing the wear and tear on furniture in our Sixth Year rooms. It would enable the speedy and efficient delivery of information to students while engaging them by the use of modern-day technology. Stress would be greatly reduced for both students and teachers.

Thank you for taking the time to consider this proposal.

Niall Ormonde.

Word Power

Close analysis of the language used in this sample provides a greater understanding of how to write effective proposals.

Compare the **different styles of language** used in the email and attachment above. Consider which text is more formal, factual, informal, personal, etc.

Study the **ideas** presented in the attachment.

(a) What is the problem and why would those addressed not be aware of it?

(b) What details are given about this problem?

(c) What is the aim of this proposal?

(d) Note that specific information is given in the proposed solution for the purchase of blinds from a particular supplier.

CLASS/HOMEWORK EXERCISE

QUESTION B

Write a proposal, to be submitted to the relevant authority (e.g. your local council or a national body), suggesting the commemoration of a woman or man who, in your opinion, has made a significant contribution to Ireland either in the past or present. Explain why you feel this person should be commemorated and suggest what form the commemoration might take. (50)

Allow about 35–40 minutes and aim for at least 450 words.

Prompt!

- **What do I have to write about?** Someone who has made an important contribution to Irish life, past or present.
- **What shape should this be?** A proposal.
- **To whom am I speaking?** A local or national body.
- **Who am I as speaker?** A teenager who admires this person.
- **Register?** Formal, concise, factual and persuasive.

Sample plan for proposals

- State your **purpose** clearly.
- Give some **background** information about why you are proposing this person.
- State a **solution** to the problem/how it can be done.
- Include **details** about costs and/or a timeline.
- Conclude by re-stating the problem, the **proposed solution** and your thanks for your proposal's consideration.

Remember!

A proposal is a formal way of putting forward an idea and requesting that appropriate action should be taken.

LESSON 25: REPORTS

Learning aim: To write an effective research report

- Essentially, reports are usually concise documents that are written for a particular purpose and audience.
- They generally communicate information that has been compiled as a result of research and analysis, often making recommendations for future action.
- Reports are factual papers that should be clear and well-structured.
- It is important to use an appropriate formal tone, avoiding personal opinion, slang, colloquialisms, jargon and clichés.

Sample Report

QUESTION B

As a member of the Green Flag Committee, you have been asked by your principal to write a report on the litter problem in the Junior School. The report will then be presented to the Board of Management.

Report: Winning the War on Litter

To: School Principal and Board of Management

From: Noel Murphy

Commissioned by: Padraig Kilburn, Principal, St Enda's Community College.

On behalf of: Board of Management, St Enda's Community College.

Date: 28th September

Introduction

The purpose of this report is to examine the litter problem in St Enda's Junior classes and to suggest possible solutions.

Research Methods

The Green Flag Committee, with the assistance of TY, organised three questionnaires (copies in Appendix) which were answered by all the Junior students, the teaching and ancillary staff.

Main Findings

- 40% of the litter is paper. 60% consists of discarded food and drinks bottles.
- There is currently no regular cleaning rota in operation.
- Litter bins are located in all classrooms, school corridors, toilets and recreational areas.
- 20% of the students regularly present without textbooks and rely on photocopies for their schoolwork. Many of these copies are discarded at the end of class.
- 35% of the students skip breakfast and go to the canteen before first class. Food and drink is often unfinished in the rush to class and thrown away.
- This practice is replicated at mid-morning break when food wrappers, cans and bottles are discarded.
- 30% of students say that they have regularly discarded gym gear, art equipment and project work.
- Ancillary staff have complained about the refusal of some students in certain classes to put their chairs on their desks to facilitate a thorough cleaning of the classrooms at the end of the school day.

Conclusions

Having examined the litter situation in the Junior classrooms through the means of questionnaires to teachers, ancillary staff and students, it has been established that there is a serious litter problem that needs to be addressed by students, staff and parents.

Recommendations

- The SPHE teacher could have a greater role in ensuring that there is a class cleaning rota in operation in each of the Junior classes.
- Students who present without their textbooks to more than three consecutive classes should receive an appropriate sanction.
- Students accessing food from the canteen before the first class should consume the food on the premises in the extensive facilities there. School prefects should be in attendance to monitor this.
- Extra storage space needs to be provided for gym gear and project work.
- Before leaving classrooms at 3.50 p.m., all students should put their chairs on the tables. This should be overseen by the teacher of the last class each day.
- The Parents Council should add a reminder to parents in the School newsletter about the importance of a good breakfast to students' health and performance.
- The Green Flag Committee should organise an educational programme to combat littering and to encourage students to maintain a clean and healthy school environment.

Acknowledgements

Thanks is due to the TY students, the members of the Green Flag Committee and the school staff for their assistance in distributing, gathering and collating the questionnaires.

Appendix

Three samples of questionnaires.

Checklist

- ☐ Use formal language and the full form of words.
- ☐ Do not give personal opinions.
- ☐ Reports are based on research (surveys or questionnaires) rather than observation.
- ☐ Avoid using the pronoun 'I'.

CLASS/HOMEWORK EXERCISES

Which of the following sentences are appropriate for report writing?

(a) Parents must give their kids breakfast.

Or

(b) Parents should ensure that their children have had a good breakfast.

Which of the following sentences are appropriate for report writing?

(c) Loads of students skip breakfast.

Or

(d) 37% of Junior School students do not eat breakfast.

Which of the following sentences are appropriate for report writing?

(e) The Green Flag Committee watched the Juniors throwing paper around.

Or

(f) All surveys showed that there were over-flowing paper bins at the end of the school day in the Junior classrooms.

Which of the following sentences are appropriate for report writing?

(g) I think there is a massive problem with litter in Junior school and it's a total disgrace.

Or

(h) Through extensive surveys over the past two years, it has been established that there is a serious litter problem in the Junior School.

QUESTION B

Write a report, to be submitted to the relevant authority (e.g. local council or Tidy Towns Committee), detailing the litter problem in the vicinity of your school and suggesting a clean-up task force in cooperation with the authority. (50)

Allow about 35–40 minutes for Question B and aim for at least 450 words.

Prompt!

The layout and format of reports vary, but most include the following:

Title: Name of report, date, author, who commissioned it and for whom.

Intro: Explain problem, why the report is being written, the terms of the report, how main ideas are arranged, who did the research and the methods used.

Body: Facts and findings can be sub-divided or bullet-pointed.

Conclusion: Summary of what the report examined and its main findings.

Recommendation: What should happen as a result of the report.

Appendix: Questionnaires, surveys, graphs, tables, visuals, etc.

Acknowledgement: Thanks to others who assisted in compiling the report.

LESSON 26: NEWS REPORTS

Learning aim: To write an effective newspaper report

News reports convey information to a particular audience but they use a different format to memos or research reports. The tone is usually detached and objective. Reports written for newspapers are written in factual language to inform readers about events that have been happening in their local area, or about national or international news. The sample plan below shows the typical news report structure.

- **Headline** – catches attention, sums up story
- **Byline** – writer's name and speciality
- **Placeline** – where the story begins
- **Key Questions** – who, what, where, why, when and how
- **Body of Report** – details, facts, quotations

Sample News Report

Sunday Independent

SUNDAY BUSINESS

Facebook's Messenger is right on the money

Steve Dempsey

IN 2012, FACEBOOK publicly warned that it wasn't doing so well when it came to mobile revenues. The social network announced that it didn't 'directly generate any meaningful revenue from the use of Facebook mobile products' and that its ability to do so successfully was unproven.

Fast-forward four years and Facebook has certainly proved it can tap the mobile goldmine. Mobile advertising revenue accounted for around 80pc of ad revenues for the fourth quarter of 2015, up from 69pc of advertising revenue in the fourth quarter of 2014.

A ruthless focus on following the users away from desktop and onto mobile platforms has been key to this turnaround. But the shift to mobile has brought with it an interesting schism.

On the one hand, there is the feed-based public platform – the Facebook everyone knows and loves – while on the other hand, the likes of WhatsApp and Facebook messenger are growing in importance. These more private and personal digital products increasingly seem like they're at the cutting edge of the online communications.

But perhaps the greatest indication of how Messenger and its ilk are growing in influence is to be found in the new news app from Quartz. The app turns the act of reading the news into a Messenger-like conversation.

'Good morning,' it said to me on Thursday morning, then followed up with: 'Brazil's ex-president, Luiz Inacio Lula de Silva, has been formally accused of money-laundering.' The message came up with a photo of the former Brazilian president. I had the options to reply with 'tell me more' about de Silva – or 'next' to skip to the next story.

If imitation is the sincerest form of flattery, Facebook Messenger and WhatsApp – not to mention other influential chat apps like WeChat and Line – should be very flattered. They are creating ecosystems for more than just chatting privately with peers. They are building platforms that have the potential to become huge commercial money-spinners, which can offer services and information via a basic interface – a conversation.

Word Power

Close analysis of the structure and of the language used in this sample provides a greater understanding of how to write effective news reports.

The headline is **short and snappy** (for a business news section) and is designed to attract the reader's interest.

Paragraphs are also punchy, giving information in a clear and concise way. The 2012 Facebook context provides a **background** for this story.

The main idea of the report (that the way we receive news is being transformed by technology) is introduced early on and then developed in subsequent paragraphs. A **specific example** of news app content lends authenticity.

Statistics are effective – but not overly-used. Language is straightforward and accessible. The report unfolds at a **lively pace** and in a logical step-by-step fashion.

Use of the present tense adds **drama** and gives a sense of immediacy.

CLASS/HOMEWORK EXERCISE

QUESTION B

1. The editor of a website aimed at teenagers is looking for articles about the changing world of either technology or fashion. Write a news report about some of the changes and innovations that are making an impact on your lifestyle. (50)

Allow about 35–40 minutes and aim for at least 450 words.

Prompt!

- Focus mainly on one key development or innovation that you have observed.
- How has this affected the world of fashion or technology?
- What has been the impact on life for you and others?
- Are there other viewpoints – 'pros and cons'?
- Would it be worth including one or two short interviews?
- Aim for clear, simple language.
- Your audience will expect you to be knowledgeable and convincing.

CLASS/HOMEWORK EXERCISE

QUESTION B

2. Imagine that a group of concerned families in your area is protesting outside your school about dangerous traffic congestion on the street facing the main entrance. You are a reporter with a local radio station. Write the text of a news report about the protest, which is to be delivered on the station's main evening news bulletin. (50)

Allow about 35–40 minutes and aim for at least 450 words.

Prompt!

- Your report should communicate the facts of the case as known.
- Include any conflicting viewpoints.
- Would it be worth including one or two short interviews?
- Mention possible developments in the story.
- Aim for clear, simple language that helps listeners to 'visualise' what you are describing.
- Your audience will expect you to be authoritative and knowledgeable.

LESSON 27: BLOGS

Learning aim: To write an effective blog

* A blog (short for 'web-log') is an online diary used to share views and experiences, offer advice and to satisfy the need people have to connect with the online community.
* Blogs have all kinds of purposes. As well as being personal diaries, they can focus on anything of interest – music, current affairs, entertainment, cooking, sport, fashion, travel, reviews, etc.
* Blogs often include lots of visuals, video clips and links to other web pages.
* As a Comprehending B task, creating a blog is similar to writing a newspaper article opinion piece.
* A blog needs to have instant appeal. Research suggests that very few people read websites word for word, so blogs need to be easily scanned.

Prompt!

When writing a blog, make it scannable by:

- having a title that pops up easily in a search
- focusing on one central idea
- employing headings and sub-headings
- using lists and capitals
- underlining to emphasise points

SUCCESSFUL BLOGS...

- Successful blogs are usually personal and address readers directly.
- They may not have a clear audience other than anyone who's interested.
- An attention-grabbing title is important. Give specific detail, e.g. 'How to' posts are usually very effective.
- A good blogger respects the reader by giving what was promised in the title.
- The tone of blogs is usually chatty, interesting, friendly, informal and informative.
- Blogs can also be used by organisations to communicate with their audience.
- To keep a regular following, good blogs are updated regularly and respond to events as they unfold.

Remember!

Always focus on producing a blog that's great for your readers.

Sample Travel Blog

RSS

6 COMMENTS

How To Avoid Being Ripped Off By Taxi Drivers

It happens. Travellers get ripped off. And it happens often.

One of the most common ways of getting ripped off involves taking local transportation and sometimes it seems as if we spend hours every single day trying to negotiate taxi or rickshaw or tuk-tuk fares wherever we go. And somehow, no matter how hard we try, we almost always end up paying infinitely higher prices than locals.

Of course, as soon as we find ourselves being ripped off or once we learn that we paid much more than other travellers for the same journey, we are oh-so-quick to place all of the blame on the evil taxi or tuk-tuk (three-wheeler) or bicycle rickshaw driver who took our money. After all, didn't we approach the driver with a smile on our face, hand them a piece of paper with our destination scrawled in local script and then, just as our guide book instructs us to do, attempt to reach an agreement on the price before we entered their vehicle?

Yes, that's exactly the steps we are trained to take and yet, we repeatedly find ourselves frustrated when the driver quotes us an extraordinarily high price for what we believe to be an extraordinarily short journey. Twenty-five dollars for a ride to the market? Come on, that's a rip-off! It's a good price sir. That's ridiculous, I'll give you five dollars. Five dollars? Impossible. Twenty dollars is my final offer. Are you nuts?

No sir, fifteen dollars and we leave now. Fine, let's go.

Eventually, too frustrated and tired to participate in this argument any longer, we accept the inflated price, climb into the vehicle and then proceed to spend days afterward moaning to every other traveller we meet about how everyone is trying to rip us off.

The Myth Of The Broken Taxi Meter

After eleven years of traveling, and I do admit that I only figured this out quite recently, I made a discovery that, for the most part, instantly eliminates the chances of me paying non-local, heavily inflated prices for transportation, no matter where I am in the world.

What I noticed is that it is only foreign travellers who approach taxis, tuk-tuks and rickshaws around the world and actually attempt to negotiate a price before even getting into the vehicle. If you take a moment to look around you, the locals in most places do not follow this method. Instead, they simply enter the taxi or step into the rickshaw and tell the driver their destination.

And off they go... with that all-too-infamous broken or missing taxi meter that all of us travellers are constantly reminded of, miraculously working just fine.

Any taxi experiences to share or advice to add? What method do you use to try and avoid paying higher fares while traveling?

www.wanderingearl.com › Blog

Word Power

First impressions are important.

When posting blogs, **titles are what sell the content**. Titles represent content in search engines, email or social media. They need to be short, simple, grab attention and meet a need. They ask the question readers are asking themselves – and immediately answer it.

The title '10 Of Our Favourite Brands on Snapchat' is short and meets a need, but lacks appeal. '10 Brilliant Brands Who Are Killing It On Snapchat' uses alliteration and a vivid verb to **catch the reader's attention**, so this link is more likely to be clicked.

CLASS/HOMEWORK EXERCISES

1. The following are examples of ineffective blog headlines. Some are not specific, others are too long, do use capitalisation or lack instant appeal. Identify the flaws in each title and write an improved version.

(a) '10 Things I Wish I Knew About Internet Marketing When I first Set Out As A Blogger Almost 3 years Ago'

(b) 'The Most Common Tips for Social Exposure'

(c) 'A handful of ways to optimise your site'

(d) 'A Blog About Stuff'

(e) 'The Absolute Best Software Ever Created'

2. Identify the elements that make this title successful, 'Snapchat Success: 10 Inspiring Brands Who Just Get It'.

3. Write a post for your blog (150 words) in which you outline the problems a young backpacker might face if touring around Ireland for the first time and give some helpful advice on how to get the best from a visit here.

QUESTION B

Write a travel blog that records your first summer holiday without your family. Describe your feelings about family holidays, how you looked forward (or not) to striking out on your own, what happened on your latest holiday and what advice you have to offer others in the same situation. (50)

Allow about 35–40 minutes for Question B and aim for at least 450 words.

Successful blogging is not about one time hits. It's about building a loyal following over time.

Sahil Saini

COMPOSING

COMPOSING

The Composing section is the most important on the Leaving Cert English paper and is worth 100 marks (25% of the overall total). The question provides an opportunity to display a variety of writing skills and a flair for language use.

Aim for 900–1,000 words (written over 80 minutes or so).

The most common compositions include:

- Personal essays
- Newspaper/magazine articles
- Persuasive speeches
- Short stories
- Descriptive essays
- Informative talks/essays

The **extended composition** will usually be suggested by the general theme of the paper and associated with a particular language genre: Most of the genres (types) of designated language use will be included among the composition titles on the paper:

* **Information**
* **Argument**
* **Persuasion**
* **Narration**
* **Aesthetic**

N.B. 'It is accepted that to classify language in this way is artificial. The general functions of language outlined here will continually mix and mingle, within texts and genres. So, there can be an aesthetic argument, persuasive narrative or an informative play.' (DES English Syllabus).

HOW THE COMPOSING QUESTION IS MARKED

Marks awarded by reference to the **PCLM** criteria for assessment:

- P = Clarity of Purpose: 30 marks (30%)
- C = Coherence of Delivery: 30 marks (30%)
- L = Efficiency of Language Use: 30 marks (30%)
- M = Accuracy of Mechanics: 10 marks (10%)

Clarity of Purpose
In assessing Clarity of Purpose, examiners will judge how successfully the candidate has addressed the question and engaged with the set task. This refers to the quality of engagement, relevance, focus, originality, and understanding of the appropriate genre.

The marks awarded for Coherence of Delivery and Efficiency of Language Use will not normally be higher than Clarity of Purpose.

Coherence of Delivery
In awarding the marks for Coherence of Delivery, examiners will assess how well the candidate has sustained the response and developed the entire answer. This refers to the quality and management of ideas, supporting points, sequencing, and engagement with texts.

Efficiency of Language Use
Marks for Efficiency of Language Use are awarded for the management and control of language. This refers to the quality of language used to achieve clear communication in terms of vocabulary, paragraph structure, syntax, punctuation, fluency, style and expression.

Marks for Language Use are awarded in so far as the candidate's answering is considered appropriate to the delivery of the task.

Accuracy of Mechanics
Marks awarded for Accuracy of Mechanics refer to spelling and grammar, appropriate to the register. Marks for Accuracy of Mechanics are essentially independent of marks awarded for Clarity of Purpose, Coherence of Delivery and Language Use.

LESSON 28: PERSONAL ESSAYS

Learning aim: To write successful personal essays

A personal essay explores your own thoughts and feelings about a subject or issue that interests you. They are usually **reflective**, allowing you to express your outlook or explain your point of view.

Personal essays also include **discussions, arguments and discursive writing** in which you give your views on issues affecting young people, such as education, media, science, relationships, sport, conflict, Irish life and culture, etc.

A strong sense of the 'first person' should be evident. However, you should avoid the temptation to couch your response completely as a personal narrative. It is important to remember that a good personal essay is not simply an account of an experience.

Personal essay titles vary greatly and can include **opinion pieces** and **newspaper/magazine articles**.

NOTE: It is essential to use the appropriate genre when writing a personal essay. You will be heavily penalised if your essay reads more like a short story or a persuasive speech. Leaving Cert 'Personal Essay' titles are unlikely to expect mere reflection, but the reflective element should play a significant part. As with all other compositions, you will be including language from several genres, such as information, description, etc.

Sample Personal Essay 1

'Be sure you put your feet in the right place, then stand firm...'

Write a personal essay in which you explore your sense of what a particular place means to you.

1. *As a fidgeting eight-year-old, I was regularly escorted to the graveyard in Drumcliffe where W.B. Yeats is buried. My mother had an interest in poetry and always had a quote ready – especially from Yeats. To be honest, I wasn't interested back then, but more recently, I have found myself wondering about the strange inscription on*

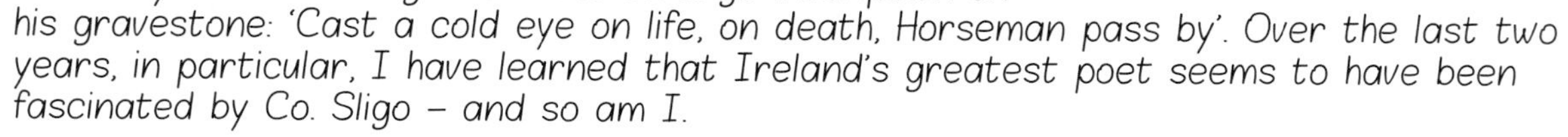

his gravestone: 'Cast a cold eye on life, on death, Horseman pass by'. Over the last two years, in particular, I have learned that Ireland's greatest poet seems to have been fascinated by Co. Sligo – and so am I.

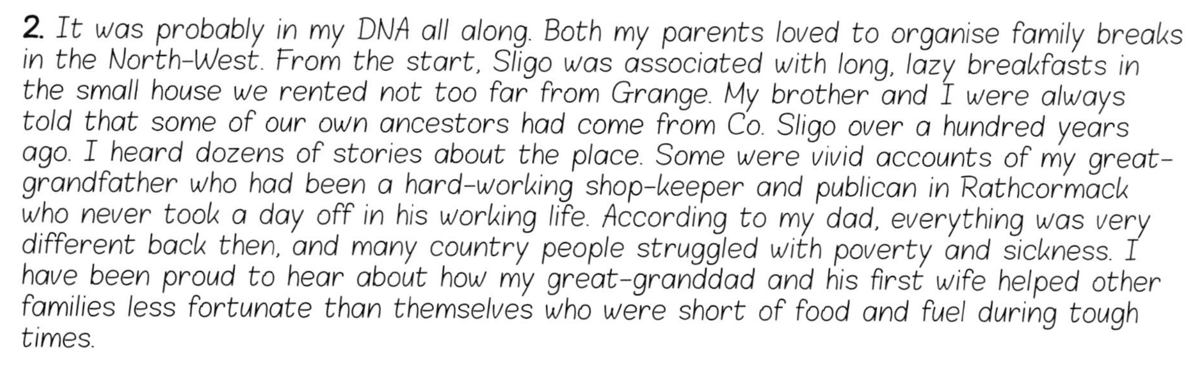

2. *It was probably in my DNA all along. Both my parents loved to organise family breaks in the North-West. From the start, Sligo was associated with long, lazy breakfasts in the small house we rented not too far from Grange. My brother and I were always told that some of our own ancestors had come from Co. Sligo over a hundred years ago. I heard dozens of stories about the place. Some were vivid accounts of my great-grandfather who had been a hard-working shop-keeper and publican in Rathcormack who never took a day off in his working life. According to my dad, everything was very different back then, and many country people struggled with poverty and sickness. I have been proud to hear about how my great-granddad and his first wife helped other families less fortunate than themselves who were short of food and fuel during tough times.*

3. *But the stories I most enjoyed were the myths and folklore of Ireland's North-West. Looking back, I sometimes half-believed that the woodlands were filled with the so-called 'little people'. I have visited a few of the magical places Yeats wrote about, including Lough Gill, the beautiful lake he was thinking about in his famous poem, 'The Lake Isle of*

Innisfree'. My aunt and cousins still live near Lough Gill in the small village where my dad grew up. Every New Year, we still go back to the old family home for a small reunion (and a fairly loud party).

4. *Perhaps this is why Sligo means so much to me. People link happy childhood memories and family life with particular places. Every time I visit Sligo, I feel a little closer to my own extended family. It's more than just gossiping and exchanging gifts, there is something extra about feeling part of a group. Although many foreign tourists come to the North-West every year to seek their roots, I myself have never felt like an outsider there. I may not know very many local people these days, but I always feel relaxed and secure enough to stroll about as if I have lived there all my life. Mum says it's all in the genes.*

5. *There is a shop in Sligo Town where a butcher gave up his old trade to begin carving wooden statues. His stunning figurines are not simple carvings but based on images of Celtic pagan warriors. Every piece is hand-made following local craft-making tradition. This man is friendly with my cousins and he can tell Irish history without any book, and recount tales of old Irish heroes and heroines. I can remember being spellbound by the adventures of King Conchobor and especially the wild exploits of Cuchulainn, the Hound of Ulster. This craftsman was also the first to interest me in the strong women of Ireland, such as Medbh, Deirdre and Aoife, usually referring to them as 'holy terrors'.*

6. *Maybe it's my over-active imagination, but Sligo seems to have more than its share of very weird superstitions. My aunt is involved in history and has shown me old pictures and drawings and old books about young boys dressed in girls' clothes. Apparently, it was an old Co. Sligo custom to deceive the fairies who were always on the look-out for young boys. Although the modern world would laugh at such behaviour, research has shown that there were higher levels of infant mortality among boys as compared to girls during the nineteenth century. It's debatable, in my view, that the fairies were ever more than people's fears. Like other legends, reality and fantasy have become blurred.*

7. *My aunt is also very well-informed about intriguing local customs to do with funerals and wakes. In the past, windows and doors were left open to let the dead person's spirit leave peacefully. A hole was sometimes made in the thatch roof for the same purpose. Sometimes the bed belonging to the deceased was carried outside to a nearby hill and burned. Strangely enough, Sligo wakes were also times for dancing and celebration. In honour of the dead, there were games, poems, singing, dancing, drinking, match-making and even wrestling contests. Needless to say, some of these parties would get out of hand and would turn into terrible scandals.*

8. *Co. Sligo is an important place and more than a link with the past. I like the look of the countryside, the dramatic coastline and I love the people. It is not just the Irish past, but my past also – and that is important. I'm not bothered by all the latest disputes about whether or not Yeats is even buried in Drumcliffe. Nor am I annoyed by the tourism and pricey coffee shops. To me, the whole county is beautiful and it has never lost its magic. From the heights of Ben Bulben, I can see Sligo Bay in its entirety. The mountain is a steep climb to the plateau above, but well worth it.*

Word count: 920

GRADE: H1

P = 28/30

C = 26/30

L = 26/30

M = 10/10

TOTAL = 90%

Examiner's comment

- Well-written, focused response.
- Clear sense of personal experience and love of Sligo throughout.
- Reflective tone is central and well-sustained.
- Effective use of description and personal anecdotes.
- Expression is varied, fluent and controlled.
- Essay is rounded off effectively, echoing early reference to Drumcliffe.

Close analysis of this sample essay provides an understanding of some of the language skills needed for writing a successful personal essay.

Paragraph 1. The **nostalgic opening tone** and use of a personal anecdote invites the reader to share the writer's reflections on childhood visits to Co. Sligo. The detail 'fidgeting' is a realistic image while 'and so am I' prepares the reader for the main body of the essay.

Paragraphs 2/3. The **focused response** continues with references to family history ('my great-grandfather', 'My aunt and cousins'), which are engaging. Place names add authenticity to the writer's reminiscences. The connection with Yeats's poetry creates further interest.

Paragraphs 4/5. Language is simple, accessible and clear. The writing has an easy **conversational fluency** ('Nor am I annoyed by the tourism and pricey coffee shops') and is very well-controlled, moving from one idea to the next in short paragraphs. Good use of a variety of lively illustrations, including local characters and mythical references, e.g.Cuchulainn, Medbh, Deirdre and Aoife.

Paragraph 6. Although there is the basis of an effective discussion point here, this is the least successful section. The idea needs to be more carefully considered.

Paragraphs 7/8. The essay gets firmly back on track with two strong concluding paragraphs. The description of the 'intriguing' customs reinforces the writer's close interest in Sligo. The **ending avoids sentimentality**, making it all the more effective ('I'm not bothered by all the latest disputes about whether or not Yeats is even buried in Drumcliffe').

CLASS/HOMEWORK EXERCISE

Write a personal essay in which you explore your sense of what a particular place means to you.

Prompt!

- Make out a short composition plan – at least five points – that will provide a basic structure for your response to this title.
- Choose a place that has a special significance for you.
- If you wish, you can model your plan on the Sample Essay above.

Composing

LESSON 29: FEATURE ARTICLES

Learning aim: To write an interesting feature article

Feature articles are written prose pieces that usually appear in the print media or on websites. They can be about any topic – from the fluffiest lifestyle human interest story to the toughest investigative report. Many news stories focus on events, but features (or opinion pieces) tend to focus more on people and issues.

These articles are not defined so much by subject matter as they are by the **style** in which they are written. Some present balanced discussions and arguments, putting forward both sides of a debate while others take a discursive or exploratory approach.

Their **purpose** is mainly to **inform**, **entertain and persuade.** They provide information, another opinion on current affairs or they present a personal or humorous perspective on modern-day life. Features offer a view into the human experience by giving more detail and description than a conventional news story. Their interest, unlike 'hard news', lasts after the publishing date because they go beyond the facts.

When writing a Leaving Certificate article for a newspaper or magazine, study the wording of the task carefully.

- **What is the purpose?** Informing, persuading, discussing, reflecting, etc.
- **Who is your audience?** Age group, gender, status, etc.
- **What register is appropriate?** Formal, informal, personal, humorous, etc.

CLASS/HOMEWORK EXERCISE

Read the following extract from a newspaper feature article about recycling and answer the questions that follow.

Recycling is a new version of religion. People do it because they feel they have to. Does anybody enjoy a trip to the recycling centre? True, we are cleansed of our filthy sinful rubbish, but who enjoys sorting printed paper from coloured magazines from cardboard? Who doesn't feel guilt at off-loading 20 cheap bottles of red vino into the bottle bank, shamefacedly explaining to any curious passers-by that they have been building up since that party at Christmas? Just like in the old days we went to confession to atone for our sins, now we go to the recycling centre to confess our guilt at wasting the resources of the earth. And just like we felt in church, we are never quite good enough. We might have a large compost heap, tote hessian shopping bags, yet nothing ever seems quite enough for the zealot wing of the recycling movement.

1. **What age group and type of person is the article aimed at?**
2. **What angle (attitude) does the writer adopt to discuss his view on recycling?**
3. **Why do you think this article will appeal (or not appeal) to many people? Support your answer with reference to the extract.**

PLANNING A FEATURE ARTICLE

Always keep the publication and readership in mind. Some of these techniques can be used to capture the reader's initial interest:

- **Question** – if the readers wants to know the answer, they must read on.
- **Anecdote** – personal and humorous stories or memories can be interesting.
- **Quote** – mostly used in personality profiles.
- **Action** – begin at an exciting moment that excites the reader's interest.
- **Description** – absorb the reader's attention with details.
- **Shock/horror** – use sensationalism to hook the reader.

CLASS/HOMEWORK EXERCISE

Read the following extract from a feature article entitled 'Sport on TV leaves Fans out in the Cold' and answer the question that follows.

Stop and think… Every three years the Minister for Communications is legally obliged to call for submissions from the general public and interested parties on what events should be on free-to-air TV. I am sure many people heard the news that sporting events were to be designated free to air and thought, 'That sounds good'. I am sure many were horrified when they heard that this move could 'kill' their sport and thought, 'Stop, I want things to stay the way they were.' Which way do you want things? What are you going to do about it?

In your opinion, is this an effective opening that entices you to read further? Support your answer with reference to the text.

Sample Feature Article

Write a light-hearted and entertaining article, for a popular magazine, that discusses how young people view the passing of time.

Marking Scheme Guidelines
Reward a clearly established and sustained register appropriate to a publication aimed at young people. Candidates may choose to adopt various approaches (discursive, descriptive, humorous, personal narrative, etc.), but expect a light-hearted, entertaining quality to the writing. Allow for a broad interpretation of 'the passing of time'.

1. 'Séan, I am not going to ask you again. Empty that dishwasher – Now!'
'Ah, Mam. I've plenty of time… I'll do it when the match is over!'

Sound familiar? Time to us teenagers is like the sky – infinite – it goes on and on and on. It just exists and it always will! While time is the enemy of our parents, who fret when a grey hair or wrinkle appears, time to us is our friend. Remember when you were given that English assignment to be ready for next Wednesday? You weren't going to do it over the weekend, were you? I mean you had to fit in Saturday morning practice, see the mates on Saturday evening, and, well, Sunday, God said it, is a day of rest. Monday, well Monday is Monday, the beginning of the week, you have to start the motor running slowly. So now it's Tuesday and it has to be in for tomorrow! What have you been doing? Well you were very busy, watching TV, playing video games, even counting the sheep in the field outside, time just melted away. Time you enjoy wasting is not wasted time. Right? Ah, but now you are not so laid-back. Do I see a faint trace of sweat on that young brow as you hunt for the given question? Will you learn from this traumatic experience as you hit Google to see what you can plagiarise, sorry, research for that assignment? Or will we have a run of Groundhog Day when you get your next assignment?

2. *Yes, Irish Mammies, the blame for this relaxed attitude lies squarely with you. Do you remember being asked by young five-year-old Séan, 'Can I please go out and play in the snow now before it starts to melt, Mammy?'*

Did you not reply, 'Not now, finish your dinner. The snow's not going anywhere. It will be there when you are finished'? And was Mammy right? Of course, she was. The snow was there, all week. Time did not creep around the corner and consume it all. So Séan learned two valuable lessons: Mammy always knows best, and there is plenty of time, all the time in the world.

3. *Séan now applies this lesson even in the most stress laden situations – exams! Given the test paper, Séan looks at the clock in the exam hall and thinks, 'Great. Three hours. No bother, I'll be done well within that time.' Séan looks around, chewing his pen, smirking at all the poor demented boys writing fifty miles an hour. Ten minutes to go, Séan is now scribbling frantically at eighty kilometres an hour, while a serene calm settles over the hall as the others quietly re-read their completed scripts! As Séan's Dad often remarked, 'Our Séan's so laid back he's almost horizontal.' Teens, learn from Séan, you do not have a magic stopwatch to pause time when you feel like it, time stops for no one. Time is what we want most, but what we use worst.*

4. *My grand Aunt Mary, always told me to concentrate on the books, not to waste time on 'distractions', boy-girl relationships. She would advice, 'You have all the time in the world for that mushy, kissy stuff 'Get on with your career, stay at the books.' I looked at her one day and I realised she was old and all she had for a companion was her cat, Mogs. She had been going out with a gaurd, but her dad had advised her she was too young to be thinking of settling down, time to concentrate on the books, get an education, get a permanent pensionable job. Times changed as did the rules, but somehow she never got round to it. The gaurd got married and had a family. How did it get so late so soon? Is there all the time in the world?*

5. *What about the brother, Pat? He's just finished his degree and announced he was on for a gap year travelling around Thailand. He decided to do an online tefal course so he could support himself when he got there, although he said that if you knew where to go you could live cheap as a bowl of rice was only 20 cents. 'You must be going to eat an awful lot of rice,' Mam said! 'Why don't you get a job? You can always go travelling when you are retired and have plenty of free time.' I thought of Aunt Mary, and although I do think Pat is dozy and I can't see him teaching the poor unfortunate Thai students his particular brand of English, 'Are youze goin' for a pint, lads?'*

6. *I did think I should row in and remind the Mam that there really is not all the time in the world. You need to travel when you are young and fit. The world is your oyster. It is full of magnificent places and people to meet. In the words of Emmet Fox, 'Do it trembling if you must, but do it'. So what about the brother? He went to Vietnam and sent an email home to say he was abseiling down a waterfall on an elephant with some*

Examiner's comment

- Overall, an ambitious attempt at an entertaining article.
- Introduction set up the thematic approach, but was over-extended.
- Reflective, personal tone is reasonably successful.
- At times, the rambling style undermined the ideas, e.g. in paragraph 5.
- Anecdotes ranged from the sharp and insightful to the laboured ('What about the brother Pat?').
- Some off-beat and light-hearted illustrations, e.g. in paragraph 6.
- Expression varied throughout from the fluent and fresh to the less well-controlled.
- Occasional flaws in mechanics, e.g. spelling errors in paragraph 4.

Israelites, but he is coming home next week, because he met an Australian in the jungle who was frying rashers, 'oh it smelt like home'! Anyway, he doesn't really like rice, can't manage the chopsticks, and by the way he'll be home next Friday and, 'Are youze goin' for a pint, lads?'

7. Now it's over to you, your turn to spill the beans. Give us your views on time and what it means to you. Share your funny experiences or stories about when you were a time-waster or where time has worked in your favour. The time deadline is Monday August 30th. Remember you may delay – but time will not. Email me at www.timeline.ie.

Word count: 973

GRADE: H2

P = 25/30

C = 24/30

L = 23/30

M = 9/10

TOTAL = 81%

Word Power

Language Style of Feature Articles

- Effective **personal tone** through use of informal, colloquial (spoken) language and first person ('I') narrative.
- Relevant jargon can add **authenticity**.
- **Facts** validate writer's viewpoints.
- Exaggeration and generalisation often heighten **humour**.
- Rhetorical **questions** involve the reader.
- **Emotive language** can evoke a reader's personal response.
- Detailed **description** adds vitality.
- Direct **quotes** personalise the topic.
- **Fast pace** with a point of interest in each paragraph and not too much detail keeps the reader involved.
- Paragraphs **flow smoothly** with transitional or connecting words ('not to mention', 'again', 'similarly', etc.).

CLASS/HOMEWORK EXERCISES

1. In the above essay, identify three stylistic characteristics of the language of a feature article and comment on their effectiveness.

2. In your opinion, is the conclusion of the feature article above satisfactory? Give reasons for your view.

Prompt!

- While introductions draw in readers, conclusions should be written to help them remember the story.
- Wrap up the story and come back to the beginning, often with a quote or surprising climax.
- Unlike hard news stories, features need an ending.
- Some newspaper articles issue a call to action.

LESSON 30: SPEECH WRITING

Learning aim: To compose an effective persuasive speech

THE PERSUASIVE SPEECH

> Speech is power, speech is to persuade, to convert, to compel.
>
> Ralph Waldo Emerson

Speeches use both the language of **persuasion** and the language of **argument** to make an impact on listeners or readers. While argument relies on a rational, logical approach, persuasion appeals more to the audience's emotions. A persuasive speech aims to convince your audience to agree with your viewpoint.

The language of persuasion is **used widely** – in school debates, political speeches, public relations' press releases, advertising, propaganda, satirical texts, and in some forms of journalism.

Pay close attention to the **purpose** of the writing task when choosing the writing style that is appropriate for a Leaving Cert persuasive composition.

NOTE: It's essential to use the appropriate genre when writing. Leaving Cert 'Persuasive Essay' titles are unlikely to expect mere persuasion throughout, but the persuasive element should play a significant part. As with all other compositions, you will be including language from several genres, such as information, narrative, etc.

Word Power

A **persuasive speech** is intended to convince the audience to do something – vote, stop littering, change their minds about an important issue – so the speech must be tailored to suit a particular audience. To communicate effectively, the writer must respect the outlook of the audience.

Persuasive texts are usually **dramatic** – feelings, images and words are shaped to manipulate the emotions and imagination of the audience in a way that is designed to bring about agreement and consent.

How do I begin?

- Know both sides of the argument.
- Know what goal you are trying to achieve.
- Know your audience – expert or novice.

Structure

- Opening statement.
- Series of points with elaboration, illustration and evidence.
- Summary and restatement of opinion.
- Call to action.

Features of Persuasive Language

- Tone (intimate, inspirational, emotive, flattering, etc.)
- Image (anecdotes, illustrations)
- Rhythm (repetition, memorable phrases, triads)
- Rhetorical questions
- Humour
- Emphatic word choice.

CLASS/HOMEWORK EXERCISES

1. Read the following extract and comment on the tone, the use of rhetorical questions and the selection of detail in this persuasive paragraph.

Persuasive Speech in Praise of Science and Technology

Let's look at an average day in the life of any person here. You were awoken by an electric alarm clock. The heating had turned itself on automatically. You had a shower, possibly heated by an immersion heater or power shower. An electric kettle boiled water for tea. The car, bus train, or even bicycle that brought you here is a product of modern science and technology. Tell me, how could we survive without these conveniences, or should I say necessities of modern life? Do you really want to return to a dish of hot water heated by the fire downstairs, (no heating in the bedrooms!), probably started at six o'clock? Do you want to walk miles to work?

2. Read the following essay extract and decide whether an appeal to the emotions or an appeal to the intellect is used to convince the audience of the wonders of science and technology. Give reasons for your response and support your view with reference to the text.

The battle against climate change and animal extinction will be won by the scientists as they patiently and painstakingly sift through evidence and draw conclusions. Recently, modern radar and video technology helped to detect a deep sea cold water reef off the south coast of Ireland. Now this area can be protected, fish and entire eco systems can be saved from over-fishing. To minimise the harmful effects of carbon emissions on the ozone layer, new sources of energy are being developed to replace oil and gas. The tall elegant blades of the wind turbines grace our windy landscape, solar panels fit snugly onto house roofs, tidal energy is being explored particularly at Larne in Northern Ireland. Our scientists and technologists are employing every means at their disposal to enhance our lives and protect our environment.

3. Based on your reading of the two paragraphs below:

(a) Identify the aim of the speaker.

(b) Select three features of persuasive language and comment on their effectiveness in convincing an audience about the importance of truthfulness in life.

If someone we trust tells us something, can we be sure that this is the truth? Well, parents start lying to their children at a very early age. From stories about Santa Claus and the tooth fairy, most parents weave a web of incredible untruths. Then when the child reaches the teenage years, the parents demand to know the truth, the whole truth and nothing but the truth. Naturally the young person, knowing that they couldn't handle it, protects himself and them by lying, and all are happy in this fool's paradise. Of course he's working hard at school, no he doesn't drink, yes he stayed over at his mate's house last weekend to help him paint the kitchen!

But, of course, relationships are based on absolute trust and truth. 'Do I look good in this? Now tell me the truth,' she demands as she twirls in front of her partner. Even a very strong man will quake at this. Should he truthfully say, 'No, dear, try something else'? Every male involved in a relationship shivers at the sharp shards of truth about to be unleashed when she says 'We need to talk'.

Similarly, the savage, biting criticism contained in some school reports paralyse the student into a scenario of 'I can't do' rather than 'I can do'. People need to focus on the positive rather than emphasising the negative, to instil confidence and self-esteem, but what about the truth? Does it become a casualty of caring?

Sample Persuasive Speech

Write a speech in which you attempt to persuade an audience that today's generation should look ahead to a brighter future instead of being sentimental about the past.

Marking Scheme Guidelines
Expect a clearly established and sustained register that uses the language of persuasion. Reward the sense of audience.

1. Ladies and Gentlemen, good evening. As Chair of the EU Initiative for Progress, it gives me great pleasure to be here this evening to open the Twenty First Century Development Conference. I know many of us worry about how modern Ireland is destroying much of what made it special, what made our country unique. Motorways through the Hill of Tara, polluted water in the West, urban sprawl and its effects on whole communities, no sense of security in our large urban centres, local post offices and garda stations being closed in rural areas. These are indeed serious issues. But I am here to challenge you not to glorify the 'cloth capped' past of history, the misty landscape of cows to market, babbling brooks, sing-alongs in quaint pubs, when a pint only cost a shilling, that's about five cents to you and me. I firmly believe that if we are to progress, we must put away our rose-tinted glasses, and be realistic about the past, the present and the future.

2. Every generation finds itself casting off the edifices of the past. Each successive generation must preserve what is best and replace what is not. This is not easy. Improvements sometimes call for harsh decision-making. Tough love. Destroying something as humble as a thatched cottage can seem almost a sacrilegious act – and yet if we had not replaced them, we would probably be cursing the dampness that would be making us shiver in the night, not to mention the hoards of scurrying mice racing across the beams! Would you want to visit the city of Rome if the Romans had decided to preserve their small shepherd's huts rather than build the spectacular Colosseum?

3. The Great Fire of London was a disaster that raged for days, burning and destroying the wooden buildings of the city. But it allowed the residents to build afresh. Christopher Wren's Cathedral could sit, pride of place, among planned roads which took people to where they wanted to go. And the old wood and wattle buildings were replaced by brick buildings which were largely fireproof and which did not harbour disease. Could they be described as lucky? Sentiment did not stand in their way. They had to start from nothing and did not have to compromise. Now before you go to get the men in the white coats, I am not advocating scorching Ireland. I am merely illustrating to you that bygone times are not always better than the future, that clinging to the past can make it impossible to reach the future. We must be bold, as well as sensitive, to what is worth preserving.

4. *You often hear talk of 'the good old days', of how things used to be better and more innocent and more fun. But were they really so idyllic? Our grandfathers wore cloth caps because they were cold and often worked outside in all kinds of weather. Most people had false teeth by the time they were in their mid-twenties. Colouring your hair was simply not an option! On a more serious note, infant mortality was extremely high, women often died during childbirth, there were little or no social benefits – and enforced emigration was the future for many. Do you really think they were such 'good old days'?*

5. *Today, we live a much better life in terms of physical health and wealth, but we today have lost some aspects of the old community way of life. Today we are time deprived. We are always just too busy to spend time. That is the challenge for our generation – how to combine the best of the present with the best of the past – and in today's conference, which I am about to declare open, we see some interesting schemes for the future, but they do demand that you spend some of your most precious asset, time. I look forward to hearing your views on our community schemes of free computer classes for pensioners, a pony club for our housing estate, a new GAA clubhouse for our rural neighbours and a life-long learning college with crèche facilities for those who wish to upskill. Our new gardening club will liaise with the Tidy Towns Committee on stand 12.*

6. *So let us not let sentimentality and nostalgia cloud our better judgement. We can make the future brighter. Seize the initiative to build a better future for ourselves and our children. It is an honour and a responsibility for us. Do not glorify the past at the expense of the future. Look forward with pride.*

7. *Thank you, ladies and gentlemen for your attention. I wish you all a wonderful few days here and I hope we will all leave the conference brimming with fresh ideas for a remarkable future. I now declare the conference open.*

Word count: 802

GRADE: H1

P = 30/30

C = 28/30

L = 27/30

M = 10/10

TOTAL = 95%

Examiner's comment

- Well-written, confident response – aptly supported.
- Controlled purposeful approach generally sustained throughout.
- Some slight loss of syntax control in paragraph 5 – overly long sentence ('That is the challenge for our generation...')
- Excellent awareness of audience – appealing to both head and heart.
- Varied sentence lengths used for dramatic effect, e.g. in paragraph 3.
- Good use of informative details and references to history.
- Rhetorical questions and repetition used effectively.
- Speech is rounded off on a positive note.

Deconstructing the Speech

Paragraph 1

Credentials of speaker are given, 'Chair of EU Initiative for Progress'. Empathy with the audience is immediately established, 'I know many of us worry'. List of worries is given to prove the speaker does understand the mindset of the audience. Announces goal – issues a 'challenge' not to glorify the past but to view it realistically as well as the present and future.

Paragraph 2
Reassuring tone conveys the message that all previous generations have cast off the past. Humorous references to scurrying mice in thatched roofs and the difference between a shepherd's hut and the Colosseum minimise the impact of tearing down old buildings.

Paragraph 3
Illustration of the potential for change for good in the anecdote about the Great Fire of London; the destruction of old buildings happened by accident, but good resulted from it. Minimising fear of the new.

Paragraph 4
Use of rhetorical questions when listing the disadvantages of the past engages the audience. Mixes both humorous and serious disadvantages of living in the past: 'false teeth', 'infant mortality', etc.

Paragraph 5
Links this disadvantage to the advantage of present good health. Repeats the challenge to keep the best of the past while moving forward to the future. Embraces the audience by asking for their contribution and allays their fears by giving a comprehensive, detailed list of new initiatives, which are coming on-stream: 'computer classes', 'pony club', 'gardening club'. Addresses fear of loss of community.

Paragraphs 6/7
Issues a call to action. Uses an inspirational tone to urge the audience to rise to the challenge, using the imperative verb, 'Seize'. Politely thanks the audience for their attention.

CLASS/HOMEWORK EXERCISE

Write a persuasive speech in which you argue for or against one of the following debate motions:

(a) **'There has never been a greater need for true equality in Irish society.'**

(b) **'Privacy is becoming a thing of the past.'**

(c) **'It's time to end Reality TV entertainment shows.'**

Prompt!

- Successful Leaving Certificate composition speeches should have a coherent central argument and a well-organised structure.
- The main aim is to convince readers by using effective persuasive techniques.

We realise the importance of our voices only when we are silenced.

Malala Yousafzai

Composing

LESSON 31: DESCRIPTIVE WRITING

Learning aim: To create vivid descriptive compositions

DESCRIPTIVE ESSAYS

> My task is, by the power of the written word, to make you hear, to make you feel – it is, before all, to make you see.
>
> Joseph Conrad

Descriptive writing provides a deeply involved experience for the reader. Its main purpose is to describe a person, place or thing in such a way that a vivid picture is formed in the reader's mind. Capturing an event through descriptive language involves paying close attention to details by using all five senses.

Just as in narrative fiction, the writer must **show**, not **tell**.

Telling:
'I slowly began to get more and more tired as the evening drew on.'

Showing:
'I leaned my head against the back of the old red armchair. The fire gently crackled and glowed. I felt my eyelids grow heavy. My breaths followed the soothing rhythm of the little clock. The room became dark and still. My eyes closed.'

This type of writing uses careful observation to reflect on the significance of what has been described. Visual and aural images to create atmosphere.

GETTING STARTED

- Identify exactly what you want to describe:
  a person
  a place
  a memory
  an experience
  an object.
- Decide on the reason why you wish to describe it.
- If you choose a person, the description should usually go beyond mere physical appearance. You might decide to show aspects of the person's character through certain details, body language, speech, and through your own direct comments.

CLASS/HOMEWORK EXERCISE

Read the following passage and write a paragraph (at least 100 words) about the effectiveness of the description. Support the points you make with reference to the text.

His great rough hands worked quickly, intricately knotting the sausages into a delicate pattern of threes, the perfect quarter pound. His blue eyes scrunched with laughter at the quick-fire banter of the other butchers. But the master butcher's deft fingers never missed a beat and the cool rectangular silver dish soon had mounds of glistening pale pink sausages ready for the rail workers' wives whose mission was to have a fry-up to get their men home with pay packet intact before the Friday night session at the pub.

NOTE: It's essential to use the appropriate genre when writing. Leaving Certificate Descriptive Essay titles are unlikely to expect mere description throughout, but the descriptive element should play a significant part. As with all other compositions, you will be including language from several genres, such as information, narrative, etc.

Sample Descriptive Essay

Write a descriptive essay based on a variety of sights observed on a journey.

Marking Scheme Guidelines

Candidates may choose to adopt various approaches (personal, narrative, humorous, discursive), but they should write in a descriptive style about a 'variety of sights observed on a journey'. The essay should contain a strong descriptive element.

1. *I take out the earplugs and put away the iPad. A spin in the Dublin rain! Bliss! On top of the 46A bus I am lord, observer of all. I look around the deck, white, strained faces are sucked into small, lit rectangular screens, 'wooed into the cyclops' eye' of virtual reality. I watch a single ice-cool steel rain drop meander down the window-pane.*

2. *I catch a glimpse of a dull, solitary, naked bulb in a first floor flat behind a dingy window, a symbol of a lonely solitary life? Had someone come to the Big City, full of hopes and dreams of the great job, finding Mr Wonderful? Was this what sad single life was like – comfortless, bleak, no warmth from another human's breath? A child cries. Students snigger. Someone behind me keeps coughing and the bus lurches over the hump-backed bridge.*

3. *The canal flowed smoothly through the sodden green verges of grass, a mirror reflecting the old statue of Kavanagh, silhouetted on his seat against the brightening evening sky, a place of redemption for the poet as he sat where nature pours 'ordinary plenty'. I discover a shimmering yellow leaf lit by the low evening sun, fluttering against the pale blue sky, suffused with all the golden warmth of past summer.*

4. *I think of my gran's old cottage in Clare, white washed walls and oil lamps. Grandad had wanted Dad to fix it up, but nothing doing, Nairobi's bustling cosmopolitan city was more his style. The cottage was like a window into the past childhood world of my mum, the old dresser full of blue and white delph, the range where Gran had conjured up mounds of fluffy white champ with melting golden centres of butter, irresistibly hot sweet apple tarts.*

'You'll burn your tongue, young son, have a bit of patience and let it cool!'

I smiled as I remembered the old settle bed with its curtain nestling in the corner of the one room house. Like Heaney's beloved Mossbawn, it radiated sunlight, serenity, 'love like a tinsmith's scoop sunk past its gleam in the meal-bin'! Its sunlit presence held the loves and laughter of others long gone.

5. *The bus shudders to a halt. I spot an old lady struggling with a collection of damp, plastic bags. She wheezes gently as she negotiates the wet bus steps. A small drama of sighs as she arrives.*

Composing

'Alright, love?' calls the bus driver.

'Sorry to be a nuisance,' she puffs.

Was she going home to her family or had they gone spreading 'their grey wing upon every tide'?

6. *I glance out onto the cold grey street. Two young lovers gaze into each other's eyes, oblivious to the whole world, content in their own. She twirls a dark curl with her finger, shyly laughing.*

'On Raglan Road of an autumn day I saw her first and knew

That her dark hair would weave a snare that I would one day rue... '

A pale frozen face comes into view, an upturned polystyrene cup held out beseechingly. Busy crowds rush by, intent on their journey home. But there is no home for a homeless person, only a hard cold pavement, no loving arm to encircle and protect, but a biting cold wind to pierce the soul as another fruitless search for a bed ends in vain. No name, no identity, just a beggar and we all pass by.

7. *My feet had grown numb under the weight of my schoolbag, plenty of homework tonight! I thought of the symmetrical beauty of the strands of DNA with their matching twenty-three chromosomes, an image of the order and beauty which surrounds us. I will delve into the 'murky' world of the power-crazed Macbeths and become a frightened voyeur as I watch Hitchcock's 'Rear Window', all scenes from other worlds.*

8. *Watching is a way of enjoying the true essence of this life with its variety and contrasts. Humans are deeply curious and a view intrigues, stimulates, makes me feel like a voyager touching another planet. I observe scenes which would have gone on, will go on, hidden and unrecorded except for a fleeting glance. My home bus-stop comes into view. I pull out my bag, pop on my earplugs and descend onto the dirty streets of Dublin, no longer the observer, but one of the crowd. The enchantment was at an end.*

Word count: 735

GRADE:H1

P = 28/30

C = 27/30

L = 26/30

M = 10/10

TOTAL = 91%

Examiner's comment

- Well-written essay with a strong descriptive emphasis from the lively opening.
- Personal tone adds to the initial sense of immediacy.
- Bus journey provides a good basis for the various observations.
- Poetry references, anecdotes and dialogue enrich the description.
- Expression is varied and fluent with effective use of verbs throughout.
- Occasionally, over-use of adjectives seems forced, e.g. paragraph 4: 'irresistibly hot sweet apple tarts'.
- Essay is rounded off effectively.

Prompt!

- To see how stories are put together, we need to deconstruct them.

Paragraph 1

The first person viewpoint establishes a quiet intimacy between the writer (the 'observer of all') and the reader. We are drawn into the writer's stream of consciousness, watching the 'single ice-cool steel rain drop meander down the window-pane'.

Paragraph 2

A closely observed solitary bulb in a window leads to a reflection on single life. The movement of the bus provides a link to the next scene.

Paragraph 3
The sight of the old canal prompts an observation about the Irish poet Patrick Kavanagh who gloried in the wonder of the ordinary.

Paragraph 4
A flashback memory to gran's homestead moves to link with Seamus Heaney, another famous Irish poet, and his thoughts about the serenity of his home place, Mossbawn.

Paragraph 5
Again, the bus's movement brings the next sight into focus. An old woman struggles with shopping. Direct dialogue is used to let the reader hear and witness the scene between the woman and the bus driver. The writer reflects on the woman's possible home circumstances.

Paragraph 6
The sight of a pair of young lovers is contrasted sharply with that of a beggar. This results in a comment about the lack of importance given to the homeless.

Paragraph 7
The reference to the schoolbag reminds the writer of homework. Now he will become an observer of the 'sights' in science and literature.

Paragraph 8
The essay concludes with a general statement about the importance of watching and close observation. The writer's and reader's vantage point of onlooker ends as the boy rejoins the crowds on the street.

A full descriptive essay does not follow the arc of a story that is concerned with the **resolution** of a conflict. It usually forms a series of pictures with some reflective commentary threaded together by a connecting link. In this case the link is the journey on the bus.

> Never trust to general impressions – but concentrate yourself upon details.
>
> From 'The Adventures of Sherlock Holmes' by Arthur Conan Doyle

CLASS/HOMEWORK EXERCISES

1. **Write an opening paragraph (at least 100 words) for a descriptive essay entitled 'A Perfect World'. Before you start, consider the following:**
   * **What do you want to describe and why?**
   * **What qualities you wish to focus on?**
   * **What sights, sounds, smells, tastes, and textures you will include to enable your reader to have this experience?**
2. **Write a descriptive essay that captures everyday life in an Irish town from the viewpoint of an observant visitor to the country.**

> A writer, I think, is someone who pays attention to the world.
>
> Susan Sontag

Composing

LESSON 32: INFORMATIVE WRITING

Learning aim: To compose an effective informative essay

LANGUAGE OF INFORMATION

> Knowledge is power. Information is liberating.
>
> Kofi Annan

The **language of information** is found in reports, journalism, web pages, instructions, letters, memos, guidebooks, leaflets, and reference books, etc. The aim, of course, is to convey information – facts and data of various kinds.

When writing to inform, the main purpose is to convey the information to the reader as efficiently and effectively as possible. The language used should be **clear, straightforward and cogent** (well organised) with a coherent structure.

Try to be as **objective** as possible, avoiding personal opinions, jargon and vague descriptions. It is not necessary to use many adjectives or adverbs, as these can often make writing subjective.

THE FEATURES OF FORMAL INFORMATIVE WRITING

Structure

- Clear opening
- General factual information about the topic
- More specific details
- Succinct summarising conclusion
- Accessible easy-to-read layout

Language features

- Factual information, statistics, etc.
- Reliable supporting reference, citing sources
- Objective, unbiased tone
- Bullet point summaries may be appropriate.

Note: Leaving Cert 'Information Essay' titles are unlikely to expect mere facts and verifiable data. For example, you might be asked to write 'an informative and entertaining article about Ireland's film industry or 'the text of a talk giving your views on part-time jobs and offering advice to students about earning money'. In both cases, you will need to include some information, but you will also be writing in other genres, such as narrative, persuasive, etc.

CLASS/HOMEWORK EXERCISE

Read the following extract and identify any features of the language of information. Refer to the tense, objective or subjective point of view, connecting words and specific detail given.

94% of Irish bathing waters have passed new stricter water quality standards introduced by the European Union. While three quarters of beaches were rated as excellent, seven beaches failed the minimum standards. The EPA (Environmental Protection Agency) measures the levels of microbiological contaminants that cause gastro-intestinal illnesses in the waters at 136 beaches and bathing areas around the country.

Sample Informative Texts

Write a magazine article aimed at giving advice to parents of young teenagers who are planning to travel abroad.

Marking Scheme Guidelines

Expect a wide range of approaches both in content and format. The information/advice may range from the practical to the personal.

EXTRACT 1

The first big trip abroad, exciting for teenagers, nerve-wracking for parents!

First hint – you'll be waiting a long time for the first phone-call home from a travelling teen. However, you do have a couple of options to keep track of your teen.

1. **Follow the money.**
Before waving goodbye, make sure you have online access to any bank or credit cards they will be using. No matter where they roam, you can monitor their transactions and make sure their account has not been hijacked. It means you can also be touched for extra funds if the teen is in difficulty with finances. Advise banks and credit card companies well in advance.

2. **Tune in to their social media.**
Most young people use their phones not for making calls, but for texting and uploading photos to Facebook, Twitter, Instagram, Snapchat, etc. Get an international data or texting plan, or swap the phone's SIM card, so that you don't end up with a huge bill.

3. **Make a copy of their travel documents.**

* Passport ID page
* Bank and credit cards
* Itinerary
* Travel insurance documents
* Flight reservations
* Train reservations
* Hotel reservations
* List of vaccinations received.

These are necessary if a person goes missing, has a passport stolen or gets robbed.

Buy your teen a money belt to keep their travel and medical documents, spare cash and/or a credit card safe. Travel and medical documents should also be loaded onto a USB stick.

4. **Pack a travel medical kit.**
Your teen should have the basics to treat sunburn, etc.

5. **Have a discussion about personal safety.**
* Keep backpacks and bags properly zipped.
* Avoid walking around alone after dark.
* Observe the laws of the country.
* Be aware that traffic rules may be different from at home.
* Do not accept food or drink from someone you do not know.
* Do not accept lifts from those you don't know.
* Be aware that laws on drink and drugs can be very severe in some countries.
* Keep personal information private from strangers.

6. **Protect with travel insurance.**
Don't allow your teen to travel without travel insurance, including trip cancellation coverage. Make sure it covers any pre-existing medical condition. Many countries are experiencing upheaval today so make sure it includes non-medical security evacuation coverage.

EXTRACT 2

Travelling is one of the great adventures in life, and should be an enjoyable experience. The only way to make sure is to plan and prepare carefully. Remember the old mantra, 'Better safe than sorry'. When travelling abroad extra preparation is needed. Make sure you have the appropriate visas and documentation. Travel insurance is a necessary expense for anyone leaving the country. It is not smart to be stranded in a foreign country, where, perhaps you don't speak the language, and you are facing a mess, perhaps a medical problem or theft. Let the insurance company take the slack. If you are taking a car abroad, join the AA. Even if you don't use it, it is peace of mind. Remember 'what can go wrong will go wrong'. Check with your friendly GP too. You may need a few injections. You will need more than comfortable shoes and sunscreen. People will want what you have so invest in a money belt too. Don't forget the credit cards and put your money in the belt. Travel insurance is necessary for anyone leaving the country too. Bon voyage.

Answer the following questions, supporting the points you make with reference to both texts.

- Which extract directly addressed the parents?
- Which extract contained specific detailed information?
- Which extract had the more accessible layout?
- Which extract struck the correct tone of reassurance?

Sample Informative Essay

Write an article for a magazine for young adult readers in which you give them advice about how to survive the pressures of dealing with their teenage children.

Marking Scheme Guidelines

The emphasis should be on advice to adults. There should be an awareness of audience. Many different approaches may be taken, discursive, narrative, humorous, etc., but the language of information should form an important element of the article.

1. *I'm sure that many adults snorted with laughter upon reading the title of this article. I know that the thought of sympathising with your teenage son or daughter after they've had a long, tough day at school is time-consuming and energy draining, right? You have better things to be doing. After all, they didn't spend forty minutes battling the commuter jam on the M50 in the pouring rain! How tough can a day at school really be? All they do is sit down at desks and pretend to be interested in a teacher's theory on why Adrienne Rich's poetry changes dramatically midway through her poetic career, or why the carbon footprint of air miles is going to totally destroy the planet!*

2. *No! There I'm afraid you are wrong. A long tough day at school can mean many things. As a parent, you know your teenager's personality; you of course had a huge influence on it. But how do you know that when your teen walks through the door that their personality doesn't change? Don't you remember everyone has a role to play in his/her class: class clown, class geek, class swot, the girl/boy who never talks? So, depending on your teen's role in class, a tough day at school can mean many things. If your pride and joy is the quiet kid who sits in the corner, have you ever thought of the struggle she faces when trying to express an opinion? How does she feel, when yet again, they are talked down by the loud, confident know-all? Every day at school is a test of character, a continual proving of who you are. So, when your daughter comes home from a tough day at school, you put down the paper, turn on the kettle and give them your undivided attention. They need your sympathy and reassurance.*

3. *I do understand that, at times, this sulky teenager morosely grunting and slamming doors can be trying. But you are the adult. He/she is the child. Teenage tantrums are to be expected, slamming doors is a rite of passage in the exploration and marking of independence. Think of it as 'I slam, so I am'. Don't retreat behind the paper muttering, 'Teenagers have never had it so good! Ungrateful cubs! Lazing around, watching TV, clearing the fridge, going to parties at the weekend.' Watch out, I see an attack of the Homer Simpson's coming on. Not every teenager is a potential Bart!*

4. *Teenagers have to cope with unheard of pressures – to conform, but be different, a neat trick! There is pressure to drink, smoke, be a certain size, achieve high points, win matches. What about the relentless exposure to media pressure? Be like this celebrity, watch how this famous person explodes, or implodes. Wear the latest label, be cool, don't be a jerk! Be a success, be famous. For what? It doesn't matter, just be famous. So, what should you do? If, by chance, they perform a chore, say thanks and mean it. If they tell you something, don't go on about 'the good old days'. Instead say something like, 'I appreciate you telling me this'. It is that easy. Give time. Give a listening, but not critical, ear.*

5. *Teenagers demand respect. You must respect their private possessions, their own space and their decisions. I understand that colouring their hair pink and having a tongue pierced can be infuriating, but have you recently looked at photos of yourself in the eighties, with your elephant flares and Afro frizz? Naturally, you as a parent will want to put forward your case, but if your son/daughter has thought seriously about* *something and still wants to do it, you have to agree. If your daughter has erected a sign on her door stating 'Laura's Room, knock before entering', you must respect this sign and with it your child's privacy. Treat your kids with respect and sympathy. The reality is that they will soon be gone. You only have a few precious years together. Spend it wisely.*

6. *We all need the reassurance that 'Somebody loves us all' – as one of our poets puts it. So, in fact, that rude, hormonal, moody person in your family just might need you as a shoulder to lean on. So, give your son or daughter the time, have the patience and help your young person to grow into the unique, young adult they have the potential to be. Do yourselves proud and remember, nobody asked to be born, nobody said it was going to be easy!*

Word count: 761

GRADE: H2

P = 24/30

C = 22/30

L = 24/30

M = 10/10

TOTAL = 80%

Examiner's comment

- Well-written essay, focused on giving advice.
- Opening clearly addresses parents.
- Sustained illustrations convey reality of teenage experience.
- Nice balance between light and serious issues (paragraphs 3 and 4).
- Advice often hackneyed and repetitive (affecting Coherence mark).
- Expression is lively, fluent and generally well-controlled.
- Essay is rounded off concisely.

CLASS/HOMEWORK EXERCISE

Write a practical Guide for Young Teenagers containing helpful advice on how to make the best of Sixth Year in school.

LESSON 33: SHORT STORY WRITING

Learning aim: To understand key aspects of narrative writing

WRITING SHORT STORIES

All writers plan their work carefully before they attempt to compose. Even a very short story, such as *Room for One More*, has a careful structure. It also includes many of the basic elements of narrative writing, such as:

- Setting
- Character
- Plot
- Conflict
- Tension
- Resolution

ROOM FOR ONE MORE

(Based on a supposedly true story from Ireland, 'Lord Dufferin's Ghost')

1. How difficult it was to sleep in that strange bed! She wrestled with the duvet, thumped the pillow; she turned her back on the flimsy curtains; she wished she had never come up to Cork.
2. At midnight she heard the grandfather clock whirr and strike; and then she heard the gravel in the driveway crunch. At once she jumped out of bed, crossed the room and peeped cautiously between the curtains.
3. A gleaming black hearse was parked outside. She peered intently, but there was no coffin and no flowers, just a crush of talking, laughing people. Then the driver of the hearse looked straight up at her.
4. 'There's room for one more,' he said. She could hear his voice quite clearly. She tugged the curtains tightly shut, jumped into bed and pulled the duvet over her head. When she woke up the next morning, she really wasn't sure whether it was all a dream or not.
5. All was quickly forgotten as shopping was planned for today. In the big store she did Levis jeanswear on the fifth floor; she did Adidas sportswear on the sixth floor and cosmetics on the seventh floor. Carrying two bulging bags in each hand she walked over to the lift. But when the bell pinged and the doors opened, she saw the lift was already jammed full with people. The lift attendant looked straight at her as she stood with her heavy bags.
6. 'There's room for one more,' he said, and his face was the face of the driver of the hearse. 'No,' she replied quickly. 'I'll walk down'.
7. Then the lift door closed with a clang. At once there was a kind of grating screech, and a terrible rattling, then a huge double thud. The lift in the big store had dropped from the top to the bottom of the shaft, and every single person in it was killed.

To see how stories are put together, we need to deconstruct them.

1. The **opening** draws in the reader using an exclamation and the adjective 'strange'. Our curiosity is aroused: why is the girl in a strange bed? Everybody has difficulty sleeping sometimes, so this detail strikes a chord with the reader. We empathise with the character as her feelings are established.

   There is also a suggestion of the girl's uneasiness. **Conflict** is a key element in any story. The setting is also established. Is she passing through Cork en route to somewhere else? The mood of restlessness is immediately created with the description: 'she wrestled with the duvet'.

2. There is a sudden noise. Notice the use of **onomatopoeia**: 'whirr'. What did the character do? Look at the vivid verbs used to describe the character's actions: 'jumped out', 'peeped cautiously'.

3. What did the girl see? Note the use of the dramatic adjectives ('gleaming black') to describe the hearse, once again heightening the reader's interest. What is unusual here? A hearse – packed with 'living people' – a detail that will be echoed later. This technique is known as **foreshadowing**.

4. The first use of **dialogue** is between the girl and the driver. It too will be repeated later in the story. The girl immediately reacts to this. Look at the strong verbs used to convey her reaction: 'tugged', 'pulled'.

5. The **time** in the story now changes. It is the next day. The **setting** also changes. The girl is out on the town. In contrast to the strange events of the night before, she is involved in a normal activity, shopping. The reader is lulled into relaxing as the different shop floors are mentioned. Onomatopoeia is again used to describe the opening of the lift door: 'pinged'. This section ends with the echo of an earlier event – the lift is jammed with people. What was jammed before?

6. Who did the girl see? Notice the repeated dialogue from earlier in the story. This is the **crisis point** in the narrative, the moment when the central character has to make a vital decision. Does she get in? The writer cleverly reveals her response through dialogue, keeping us involved in the story. It is much more effective than stating the obvious: 'She went down the stairs'.

7. This marks the **resolution** of the story. Endings can be happy or sad, but the reader must never feel cheated. Sound effects create the terrifying atmosphere – 'clang', 'grating', 'rattling', 'thud. The story ends with the lift crashing and everyone – except the girl – is killed. The suggestion hanging in the air is that the girl's dream saved her. We are not told what happened until the very last line of the story. This is how the reader's attention is held until the final moment. Only then is the tension in the story released... leaving the reader satisfied.

   The girl's name is never given. Do you think this adds to the unsettling atmosphere?

CREATIVE MODELLING

Use the following plan, based on the structure of *Room for One More*, to write a short story where a character has to make a difficult decision.

1. Introduce your main character. Establish your **mood** and setting. Suggest the source of conflict. Arouse the reader's curiosity with an unusual detail. Remember the reader must be left asking: 'What is going to happen next?'
2. **Show** the reader what happened next. There is a noise. Use onomatopoeia to let the reader hear the noise. Make the character perform an action in response to the noise.
3. **Describe** what the character saw. Use vivid details. Let the reader see what the character is seeing. Introduce an unusual angle. Remember to echo this later in the story.

4. Use **dialogue** between the two main characters to show a conflict of interests. Use this dialogue later in the story. How does your character react to this interchange? Describe the reaction of the main character, using strong verbs.
5. Change **the time and setting** in your story. Involve your reader in a normal setting to create a false sense of security. Use sound effects to convey atmosphere. End with an echoed detail from an earlier part of your story.
6. Now what does your character see? Repeat the dialogue from the earlier part of the story. Have your character make an important choice or formulate a decision. This is the climax or crisis point of your story. Let the reader know the character's **decision** though dialogue.
7. Resolution... What type of **ending** will you have? Happy or sad? The ending must come as a consequence of what your character decided. Onomatopoeia can be used to create atmosphere. Only let the reader know what happened at the last sentence. Note: The reader must be left **satisfied** with the **ending**.

The sample response below uses creative modelling to write a short story about a character who is faced with making an important decision.

Plan

1. Who is in the story? Deirdre.
2. Where will it take place? At the fun-fair.
3. When will it take place? Summer evening after end-of-year exams.
4. What will happen? The ferris wheel crashes.
5. Why will it happen? A strange accident.
6. What will the climax be? Deirdre will decide not to get on, due to a premonition.
7. How will it end? Many will be injured, but Deirdre will survive.

Sample Short Story 1

Peep, peep! Peep, peep! Deirdre stretched out a sleepy hand and killed the alarm. She opened one eye. Six o'clock! She smiled, no need for dawn starts, the dreaded Third Year exams were well and truly done and dusted. Party-time tonight! She turned over and nestled under the duvet.

A huge clatter broke the silence. Deirdre groaned. The early morning bin collection. She tugged the pink curtain and peered out. A great lurid, multi-coloured refuse lorry crushed and gnarled, twisted and screeched as the bin contents tumbled, torn and shredded in to a million pieces.

'That's all for now,' grunted the driver as he slammed the lever down. His cackling voice echoed in the still morning air. Deirdre sighed happily as she slipped gently into a soft sleep. When she woke up much later, she tried to remember what had disturbed her beauty sleep.

But no time for that now! Important matters were looming. The gang were all meeting at the Carnival later tonight for post-exam celebrations. The biggest ferris wheel in Ireland was set up at the Sportsbowl on the edge of town. It rose that evening with lurid multi-coloured lights against the darkening sky. Old Sixties music blared from the crackling loudspeakers: 'This will be the last time. This will be the last time, the last time for us all, Oh, oh!'

Deirdre excitedly paid for her ticket as she scanned the huge queue, looking for her mates. She joined the end of it anyway to bag a space. The great wheel twisted and screeched as it turned, protesting in the soft summer air. A scream rang out. It was the gang, further down the queue. She turned and waved. She was next on. The old man in the booth motioned her on the wheel as he cackled,

'That's all for now,' and his face was the face of this morning's refuse lorry driver. Deirdre shivered. 'No,' she replied quickly, 'I'll wait on my mates.'

The music continued to blare as the wheel gave a great shudder. The old man slammed the lever and at once there was a crunching, snarling sound as the great wheel slowly toppled over in a sickening slow motion. Screaming rent the air as bodies hurled twisting and turning into the tangled heap of metal, young bodies torn and shredded like discarded refuse.

CLASS/HOMEWORK EXERCISE

Using the seven-point plan above, outline another version of the 'Room for One More' plot. Create a new character who is having a close escape in a different setting.

Remember!

Even the greatest writers wrote new versions of old stories.

So all my best is dressing old words new,
Spending again what is already spent.

Shakespeare (Sonnet 76)

If you steal from one author, it's plagiarism; if you steal from many, it's research.

Wilson Mizner

Read a lot and write a lot!

Stephen King

Composing

N.B. Examiners remarked positively on some candidates' skills in crafting memorable short stories. These candidates displayed confidence in their handling of elements of short story writing such as: narrative shape; effective characterisation; developing a coherent plot; attention to aspects of setting (including time, period and place); the use of dialogue and the creation of atmosphere (including the skilful use of drama and tension). Short stories are more effective when the readers are drawn into the story through the effective use of suggestion and a well-controlled narrative structure.

Chief Examiner's Report (www.examinations.ie)

LESSON 34: SHORT STORY PLOT

Learning aim: To understand how plot, tension and flashback create a successful story

PLOT

> Plot is what happens in your story. Every story needs structure, just as every body needs a skeleton.
>
> Caroline Laurence

The plot usually consists of a **beginning**, where the conflict is set up, **middle** where the story reaches its climax and **end**, where the conflict is resolved. Writers often work to a basic three-act structure: the set-up, the confrontation and the resolution. The shape of a story is an arc, rising to a crisis point for the central character and then falling away towards the end. There are countless kinds of narrative structures, but many follow some version of the classic structure shown in the plot diagram.

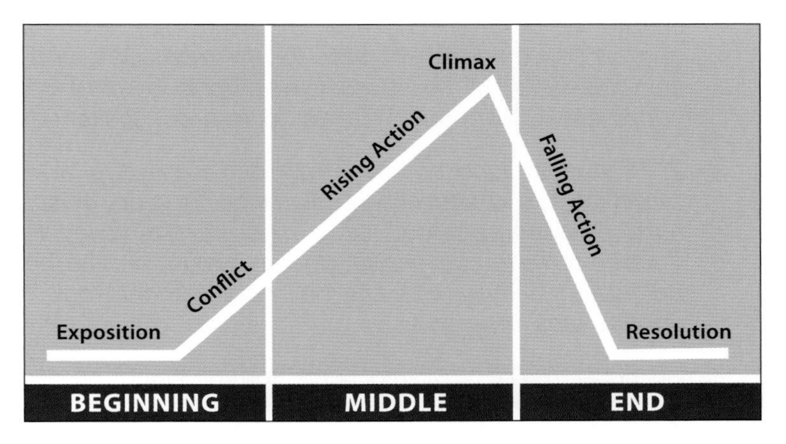

STRUCTURING A SHORT STORY PLOT

Beginning

Introduce your characters and their world. What do they want to achieve? What obstacles stand in their way?

(Remember there is no story without conflict, either between characters, between a character and his world or within a character.)

Build-up

What's going to happen? How will you build up to the climax?

(The character must have a challenge and there should be an element of risk to keep the momentum of the story exciting.)

Climax

Bring the action to a head when the main event or turning point happens. The central character will have to make a decision.

Ending

The conclusion needs to resolve the conflict either happily or unhappily. It has to leave the reader feeling, 'it should end like that'. The main character has probably learnt a lesson about life or perhaps there has been an unexpected development.

Flashback

A story does not have to be told chronologically (the order in which the events occurred). Often the writer begins the story when the character is already in a state of conflict, in mid-action, and then goes back in time to show how the character arrived at this predicament.

Sample Short Story 2

Write a short story in which the central character responds to a challenge.

Marking Scheme Guidelines

Reward awareness of the narrative shape of a short story (setting, characterisation, plot, dialogue, tension, climax, flashback, etc.) and the quality of the writing. A central character should react to a challenge or crisis.

1. *'What's it all about, Alfie? Is it just for the moment we live?' Stupid Sixties song blaring from the next bedroom, but it's a good question! What is it all about? Outside my window, a wasp's nest is lit by Dublin's evening sun, beautiful and strange, ghostly, yet wildly alive; an edifice of frail white matter glued by a paste so strong that it withstands the harsh, cruel strength of the wind. Tier after tier of filament has been laid down, one on top of another, just like my memories. And if I probe my memories or the nest too closely, I will be stung. Layer upon layer of regret, laughter, anger, joy, rage and happiness. Challenges I failed to rise to, challenges I confronted.*

2. *It wasn't good to catch my father's eye, a piercing pinprick of critical analysis, swivelling like a searchlight, illuminating every mistake. The thin lips pursed as the cold, hard phrases spat out like a machine-gun volley. He had only one love in his life, rugby. I was to make the grade, do him proud, be the best out-half since Sexton or Henshaw, operating skilfully with the ball on the front foot, fulfilling his dreams. I told him that cricket was my game.*

'Useless! You're your mother's son, all right!' he stormed. 'I'm off to the club.'

3. *Dad's real home was the left hand corner of the rugby club bar, where he always hangs out with the 'lads', Laverty, Midas, 'Doc' Jones and Jinxie, recalling the past glories of old rugby club matches. One drink follows another as each man must stand his round. The raucous laughter grows ugly as the evening wears on. The macho posturing becomes more and more absurd. Sweating round-bellied men, reliving their lost youth, swilling their frothy pints.*

4 *One o'clock, the heavy tread on the stairs said it all – a stumble, a curse, and the slam of the bedroom door. Now it begins. My mother's low-pitched voice trying to calm things, Dad's rough tones rising as the usual complaints ring out about her 'useless' son. I put on my earphones, time to tune out. Tomorrow I will be meeting the mates for cricket. My room door swings open. He stands there, breathing heavily, swaying slightly in the doorway.*

5. *'Doc's' boy has been chosen for the Under-21s. Well, pretty-boy, when are you going to play a man's game?'*

'Stop it, Coleman,' my mother's voice faltered. 'This is doing no one any good.'

'Stay out of this!'

'For God's sake, Coleman. You've just had too much to drink.'

He grabs her by the shoulders, shaking her like a little child's doll. Then an unreal blur of shadows as his clenched fist crumples her to the floor.

6. *Without thinking, I lift the cricket bat and go to rain it down on him. Fear replaces the sneer on his face. He falls to his knees. I swing the bat above my head. A sickening thud sounds as wood meets flesh and bone. The old man lies in an ever-widening red stain of blood. I'm breathing heavily now. My mother sits up.*

'Barry, Barry what have you done?'

I lift my arms to comfort her.

Composing

'Get away from me,' she snaps. 'Look what you've done! Coleman! Are you all right?'

She cradles the slumped figure of my father in her arms, tears rushing down her cheeks. Then she turns.

'You fool, you stupid selfish fool. What do you know about anything?'

7. I shouldn't have started probing into the past – but the memories are racing now. My mother springs into action, calling the ambulance, calling the Gardaí. Before I know it, the burly garda is beside me, notebook in hand.

'Now lad, tell me what happened.'

I tried. It sounded dumb, a game of rugby, a game of cricket, a challenge faced, a game of life and death, a pointless story told by a fool. The garda guiding me out to the waiting car. Everything had changed for me.

8. The sunlight spills across the worn desks as the dust dances around the English room of St. Pat's. The other lads doze as the old teacher enthuses about how the great writers shine their searchlights into the gloom showing life in all its shades of grey. Even when we rise to the challenge, we fail sometimes. Old Macbeth struck too and changed his life forever. He also figured out that life is a 'tale told by an idiot signifying nothing".

9. The mates haven't called, caught up with the Pres I expect. Mum hasn't visited, she's busy caring for Dad. He needs round-the-clock care, but he will get better. I don't play cricket anymore. I can't see the wasp's nest now the sun has gone down. The memories start to subside too. I switch on the lamp and begin to read:

'So boy, don't you turn back.

Don't you set down on the steps

'Cause you finds it's kinder hard.

Don't you fall now.'

Word count: 835

Examiner's comment

- Focused response, exploring the father-son conflict.
- Setting and uneasy mood effectively evoked.
- Central character engages readers' sympathy, e.g. paragraph 8.
- Some very good use of suggestion, e.g. paragraph 4.
- Detailed description and dialogue add authenticity.
- Narrative is rounded off poignantly, echoing the opening.

GRADE: H1

P = 28/30

C = 24/30

L = 28/30

M = 10/10

TOTAL = 90%

CLASS/HOMEWORK EXERCISES

1. Deconstruct the above story using the outline guide below to help you. Respond to each question with a sentence or two supported by suitable reference to the story.

Paragraph 1: Introduction
Where and when is the story set? Who is the main character? Is he content or ill at ease? What kind of atmosphere has been established?

Paragraph 2: Flashback
What has happened which has led to the character's predicament?

Paragraph 3: Obstacle
What is preventing the character from achieving his goal?

Paragraphs 4/5: Challenge
What else is preventing the character from achieving his goal?

Paragraph 6: Climax
Now that the tension is at its height, what decision does the character make?

Paragraph 7/8: Consequence
What has happened as a result of the character's decision?

Paragraph 9: Resolution
What has changed as a result of the character's decision? Is the conflict resolved or unresolved? Is this a satisfactory ending within the 'world' of the story?

2. Draft the plot for a short story in which the central character has a heavy burden to bear. You might wish to use some of the outline above as a guide.

Remember, 'plot' (or storyline) is a literary term used to describe the events that make up the main part of a story. These events relate to one another in a pattern or a sequence. Readers need to keep asking: What is going to happen next?

It's often said that there are only about half a dozen basic plot lines in literature:

- Rags to riches (*Cinderella*)
- Boy meets girl (*Romeo and Juliet*)
- Winning against the odds (*David and Goliath*)
- Innocent characters falling into a trap (*The Spider and the Fly*)
- Fate catching up with a wrongdoer (*Macbeth*)
- Goodness rewarded (*Sleeping Beauty*)

Word Power

In paragraph 5, the climax occurs. This is the moment of greatest tension in the story. The drunken, abusive father confronts his son and physically attacks his wife. The boy has to decide what to do. **The writer shows, rather than tells the story.**

Active verbs in the present tense, ['lift', 'swing'] describe the boy's decision, adding to the **dramatic atmosphere**. The writer places readers inside the room, listening and watching as the events unfold. We hear the onomatopoeic 'sickening thud'. Vivid imagery conveys the distressing sight of the wounded father: 'ever-widening red stain of blood'.

Dialogue also carries the momentum of the story. The reader hears the unexpected critical reaction of the mother: 'Get away from me', 'you stupid selfish fool'. By showing rather than telling, the writer increases the emotional effect.

3. Choose a paragraph (other than paragraph 5) from Sample Story 2 that you found interesting. Write a 'Word Power' commentary (at least 100 words) about the writer's use of language.

Good writing is supposed to evoke sensation in the reader – not the fact that it is raining, but the feeling of being rained upon.

E.L. Doctorow

LESSON 35: SHORT STORY SETTING

Learning aim: To create a believable setting and engaging opening for a story

SETTING

> Everything happens somewhere, sometime.
>
> James D. Carswell

Fiction has three main elements: **plot, character** and **setting**. The setting is where and when the action takes place. The writer creates a new reality that the reader enters and then takes for granted while the story and characters become more believable. Setting provides the scaffold of the narrative, making it follow a particular path. Every story would change if the writer moved the characters and plot to another time and location. Setting suggests the passage of time through weather, lighting, season and time of day. It also sets the opening mood of the story.

NOTE: It's essential to use the appropriate genre when writing. Leaving Cert. 'Narrative Essay' titles are unlikely to expect mere narration throughout, but the narrative element should play a significant part. As with all other compositions, you will be including language from several genres, such as description, information, etc.

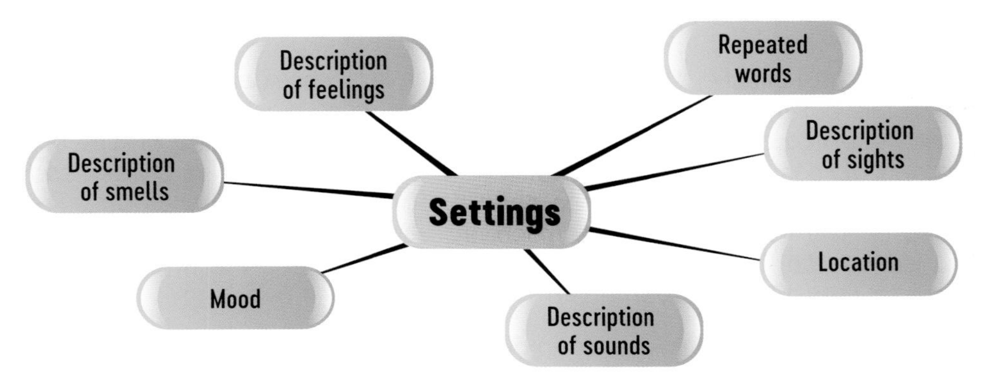

Sample Short Story 3

Write a short story in which the main character makes a decision that sets him or her free.

Marking Scheme Guidelines
Reward awareness of the narrative shape of a short story (setting, characterisation, plot, dialogue, tension, etc.) and the quality of the writing. The story should involve the gradual disclosure of the decision which sets the character free.

1. *The wind stung my cheeks as I felt the rush of speed. The bright red Porsche clung to the curves of the Californian cliff side. I felt the throb of the engine as it purred smoothly eating up the road. Up here I could breathe. Up here, I felt the adrenalin rush as the country whipped by. A slice of orange sun slipped quietly into the indigo sea. I urged the car into a higher gear. The scenery blurred.*

2. *The Porsche had begun it... 'Happy birthday, darling,' Dad had emailed. 'Hope you like your eighteenth birthday present. Business calls, what's new? But see you soon. Have a ball!'*

3. *Yeah, right, business always calls, business with a short skirt and an expensive taste in wine. But I had a ball that night at the club, until I caught the boyfriend Derry with my 'best' friend Selena, the beautiful. 'Happy birthday, darling,' Derry had said. 'Selena's not feeling well. I'm going to take her home. See you soon. Have a ball!'*

4. Selena leaned her head on Derry as they made their way out into the night. Yeah, right, like she's too sick to go in a taxi. So I did have a ball that night, me and the old booze. Good decision. Life blurred, I felt myself sinking into nothingness.
The following morning, carefully holding my enormous head which seemed to have enlarged overnight, I went to check my degree results. The college had never changed the old tradition of posting the names on the front notice board for all to see – except I couldn't see, not really. The rows of names swam in a never-ending dance. And then there it was – 'O'Connor... Fail.' Yep, that just about sums everything up. 'O'Connor... Fail.' That's me.

5. My feet began to move slowly, unsteadily at first, but then I was running up the concrete stairs, faster, faster up round the curves of the stairwell, the banisters slipped noiselessly from my view. The wind whipped my hair. I could breathe up here. I moved closer to the edge. The world looked small and of little importance from this height. I felt calm and strangely powerful in the silence. I stood swaying on the very edge.

6. 'Hey, Kid, don't do it!' A deep voice came from nowhere and two strong arms pulled me from the edge. The security man, Jack, had seen me run up and had raised the alert. 'No Jack, I wasn't going to do anything stupid. Dad's flying home tonight, just wanted some air.'

7. 'That's alright then, Miss. You really gave us some kind of a scare. He's a good man, your dad. Worked for him for almost forty years. You sure you're ok? Always very proud of his little princess, y'know.'
'Thanks, Jack, don't worry. I'm off home now.'
'You sure? Drive careful now.'
'Will do, Jack.'

8. I climbed into the Porsche, slipping into gear. 'His little princess' didn't seem to figure much in the old man's life recently. The results were right. 'O'Connor... Fail.' The speedometer began to climb steadily 70, 80, 90. Suddenly I slammed on the brakes and the car skidded across the wet grass. Not yet. I would decide when I was ready to be free. No one else. I pushed the car door open swiftly and went to the edge. The white waves danced on the rocks in the pale moonlight. A tear, one cold stupid tear ran down my cheek. I wanted to follow that single drop to somewhere I wouldn't have to think – wouldn't have to feel anything ever again.

9. 'Hey, don't do it!' Derry's strong voice rang out. Derry, the taxi driver – I didn't want to deal with him now. I did not want to think about him. I slowly turned my head. But perhaps? Had he really come? This had always been our special place, away from the world where we could dream and hope for a future together. Derry was going to have a whole chain of garages, I was going to open a crèche. Some joke, right? I caught a glimpse of the wet grass coldly gleaming in the moonlight. My eyes swam. A shadowy figure appeared. I reached out towards it...

10. 'Derry, Derry?' My foot slid on the wet grass. I was falling, falling but now I desperately wanted to live...

Word count: 731

GRADE: H2

P = 25/30

C = 23/30

L = 23/30

M = 10/10

TOTAL = 81%

Examiner's comment

- Dramatic setting and mood maintained throughout.
- Appropriate jaunty style, lively verbs and varied sentence length.
- Introspective first person viewpoint engages readers.
- Flashbacks work well.
- Some over-explanation and melodrama, e.g. paragraph 8 ('Not yet. I would decide when I was ready to be free. No one else.' 'A tear, one cold stupid tear ran down my cheek').
- Detailed description and dialogue add authenticity.
- Open-ended conclusion may not convince some readers ('I was falling, falling but now I desperately wanted to live...')

CLASS/HOMEWORK EXERCISES

1. Study the opening of the above story.
   (a) Write a paragraph (at least 100 words) describing its setting and mood.
   (b) What expectations does it set up for the reader?
2. Read the following two descriptions and answer the questions that follow.
   (a) Heavy blue-black bruised clouds hung in the sky. Squalls of rain flung themselves at the cliff. The wind moaned. Enclosed in the shelter of my car, I shut my eyes and the memories flooded back.
   (b) The wild squeals of children filled the air, as they tipped their toes gingerly in to the icy blue waves dancing on the gleaming white sand. The hurdy-gurdy sound of the ice cream van droned and the sun baked the rows of glistening brown bodies. I leaned back, lazily, and took a deep breath as I stared into an ever deepening blue sky.
   (i) Describe the mood in each of these descriptions.
   (Suggestions: happy, sad, foreboding, relaxed, sinister, uneasy, calm, tranquil, etc.)
   (ii) Pick out two phrases from each setting that create the mood and comment briefly on the effectiveness of the language. (Focus on the choice of adjectives, strong verbs, and the appeal to the senses.)

OPENINGS

The opening introduces the characters as well as the setting. It also begins to develop the strands of the main plot. There has to be some **hint of conflict**.

A character in mid-action is likely to capture the reader's interest. Decide whether you want your story to be comfortable or uneasy. What is the weather, the time of day, the mood?

An intriguing opening will make the reader want to read on…

I snuggled happily under the warm duvet. Leaving Cert. done, parents on holiday, the house entirely to myself, life was good. A faint noise sounded from the hall downstairs. Just the wind, I thought as I turned over. But there it was again, a steady series of creaks coming nearer, moving up the stairs…

The reader is engaged. Who is on the stairs? What is going to happen next? Will there be a robbery – or worse?

Always aim to make the opening interesting. It is best to involve your reader through suggestion rather than explaining everything.

One day, Mark walked along the road to Linda's house. He was really hoping he might see her by chance. He just wished that she would take some interest in him.

The writer is 'telling' the story rather than 'showing' it. How could it be improved?

The grim, grey road stretched endlessly in front of Mark on yet another chill autumn evening. The freezing wind stung his face. He pushed his hands deeper into his jacket pockets as he struggled to catch a glimpse of Linda's house through the sheets of driving rain.

Notice how the writer is setting the scene – using the weather to suggest Mark's miserable mood. Alliteration ('grim, grey') and strong verbs ('stung', 'pushed', 'struggled') suggest his effort to catch a glimpse of Linda.

CLASS/HOMEWORK EXERCISE

1. Read the following opening and then write a paragraph (at least 100 words) commenting on two features which you thought made it effective.

There were no lights in the bike shed. The surrounding bushes loomed menacingly in the November twilight. A slight rustling came from the left corner. For an instant, John caught a blurred movement from the corner of his eye. He turned, breathing harder, and there it was… a small white hand parted the bushes. John turned quickly…

Prompt!

- The opening of the story must create a believable world in which the events will unfold in a particular setting.
- It usually introduces the main character and the possible conflict.
- There will often be a sense of the initial mood, either relaxed or scary.
- The opening leaves readers intrigued, asking questions.

FAMOUS OPENING LINES

As a boy, I wanted to be a train.

Machine Man by Max Barry

It was a bright cold day in April, and the clocks were striking thirteen.

1984 by George Orwell

Once upon a time and a very good time it was there was a moocow coming down along the road and this moocow that was coming down along the road met a nicens little boy named baby tuckoo.

A Portrait of the Artist as a Young Man by James Joyce

I will begin the story of my adventures with a certain morning early in the month of June, the year of grace 1751, when I took the key for the last time out of the door of my father's house.

Kidnapped by Robert Louis Stevenson

I write this sitting in the kitchen sink.

I Capture the Castle by Dodie Smith

There was no possibility of taking a walk that day.

Jane Eyre by Charlotte Brontë

When I was a young lad twenty or thirty or forty years ago I lived in a small town where they were all after me on account of what I done on Mrs Nugent.

The Butcher Boy
by Patrick McCabe

The schoolmaster was leaving the village, and everybody seemed sorry.

Jude the Obscure
by Thomas Hardy

As Gregor Samsa awoke one morning from uneasy dreams he found himself transformed in his bed into a gigantic insect.

The Metamorphosis
by Franz Kafka

IN THE BEGINNING, THE UNIVERSE WAS CREATED. THIS HAS MADE A LOT OF PEOPLE VERY ANGRY AND BEEN WIDELY REGARDED AS A BAD MOVE.

THE RESTAURANT AT THE END OF THE UNIVERSE
BY DOUGLAS ADAMS

Having placed in my mouth sufficient bread for three minutes' chewing, I withdrew my powers of sensual perception and retired into the privacy of my mind, my eyes and face assuming a vacant and preoccupied expression.

At Swim-Two-Birds
by Flann O'Brien

IF YOU REALLY WANT TO HEAR ABOUT IT, THE FIRST THING YOU'LL PROBABLY WANT TO KNOW IS WHERE I WAS BORN, AND WHAT MY LOUSY CHILDHOOD WAS LIKE, AND HOW MY PARENTS WERE OCCUPIED AND ALL BEFORE THEY HAD ME, AND ALL THAT DAVID COPPERFIELD KIND OF CRAP, BUT I DON'T FEEL LIKE GOING INTO IT, IF YOU WANT TO KNOW THE TRUTH.

THE CATCHER IN THE RYE
BY J.D. SALINGER

For the better part of my childhood, my professional aspirations were simple - I wanted to be an intergalactic princess.

Seven Up
by Janet Evanovich

CLASS/HOMEWORK EXERCISE

Having read the above opening lines, choose one which intrigued you and write a short paragraph (100 words approx.) explaining your choice.

LESSON 36: SHORT STORY CHARACTERISATION

Learning aim: To understand characterisation and to create credible fictional characters

CHARACTERISATION

> You take people, you put them on a journey, you give them peril, you find out who they really are.
>
> Joss Whedon

> I try to create sympathy for my characters, then turn the monsters loose.
>
> Stephen King

Characterisation refers to the **creation and development** of fictional characters. Writers usually present memorable characters through their physical appearance and through their behaviour – what the characters say, think and feel and what they do or do not do.

Readers also learn about characters from the reactions of others and from the author's direct **narrative voice**.

Leaving Cert. short stories are very short (900–1,000 words) leaving little time to fill in a character's backstory and show his/her personality. The main purpose of the examination story is usually to develop a single **central character**.

Successful authors give us just one or two **significant details** when portraying a character. The Victorian novelist Charles Dickens created some of the most memorable fictional characters. In *Great Expectations*, he describes a bitterly unhappy woman who was once jilted at the altar. Miss Havisham 'had but one shoe on'. This detail quickly shows how her life stopped at the very moment she heard that she was no longer going to be married.

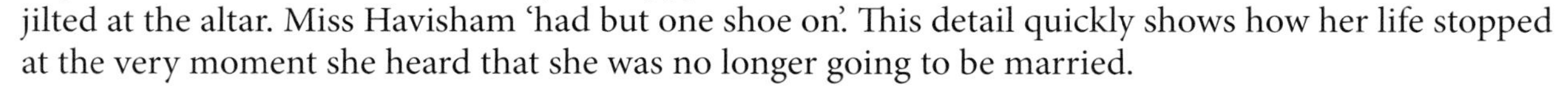

Dickens describes Miss Havisham's face through the detail of the 'brightness of her sunken eyes'. She is a **haunting figure**, dressed all in white, but of a white which had long ago 'lost its lustre, and was faded and yellow'; a cross between a waxwork and a skeleton. She is presented as a woman in perpetual mourning, but still full of energy, determined to take revenge against all men because of what happened to her.

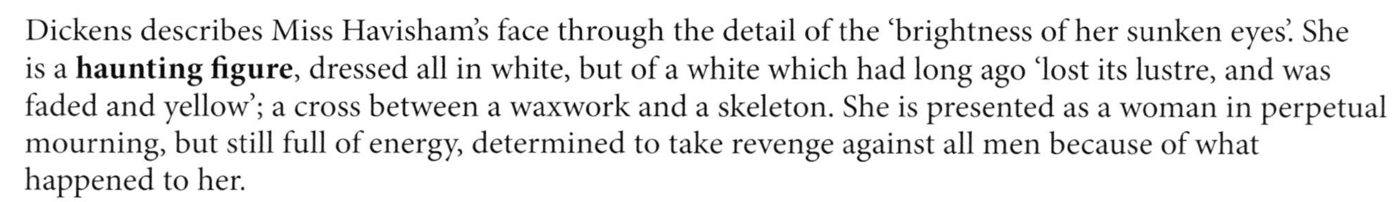

Composing

DESCRIPTION

'The legs were tucked into new white football socks, neatly folded at his ankles. Mr. Percy's football boots were polished as black and shiny as the bombs used by assassins in comic strips.' From *A Kestrel for a Knave* by Barry Hines

This short description paints Mr. Percy as a foolish character while comparing his boots with bombs also links him with danger.

Sample Short Story 4

Write a short story in which a young person is eager to be independent.

Marking Scheme Guidelines
Reward awareness of the narrative shape of a short story (setting, characterisation, plot, dialogue, tension, climax, flashback, etc.) and the quality of the writing. A central character's life should change as he/she attempts to be more confident and independent.

1. *I'd got it! My new summer job was in the bag and I was delighted. I had tried two different farmers – no joy, and I was going to look for a different job, but I kept trying and I got my just desserts. I was driving a tractor for the summer. Many people thought I was stupid, but I was in it for the money. Sixty euro a day, long hours, but it didn't dishearten me. I may look small for my age, but I'm strong and not afraid of hard work.*

2. *On June 12th I started. I arrived at the yard at ten to nine, ten minutes early. This gave me the opportunity to look around and familiarise myself with my new surroundings. I checked out the machinery and the workshop and at five past nine, the boss, Kevin O'Brien, arrived. Within minutes the whole crew was there and I was shown which tractor I would be driving. I wasn't impressed! Rusty, slow and dangerous would be a kind description of this tin can, but nevertheless I got on with it. One of the more experienced drivers showed me how to drive alongside the silage harvester and fill the trailer as well as how to tip the load. After about two loads, I was on my own. We finished the first field no bother, but the next field was about two miles up the road. This was where the trouble started.*

3. *I filled my trailer alright, and everything was going fine, until I came to the driveway of the yard. I couldn't stop. I pressed and pressed the brake, pumping it until I thought my foot would go through the floor and then it shuddered to a stop.*

'Oh God!' I muttered as I wiped the sweat from my face.

I reversed slowly back up the driveway and into the yard. I was glad it was deserted.

4. *A few days passed without any problem, and I began to get to know the others. I met a lad named John, who was the same age as me. It was his second year working with Boss O'Brien, and he was well liked, so much so that they gave him a nickname, 'Towney'. I hoped we'd be pals. At first I didn't get it, but it was because he never left town, always lapping the streets in his Honda Civic. We had another road draw on Wednesday, a week later, and by this stage I was friendly with all the other boys, and every time we met on the road, there'd be light-flashing and hand-waving. I even had a new baseball cap which I took off to salute them.*

5. *But on that same day I lost a bit of concentration. Just when I thought I was getting used to the long hours and the old tin can tractor I hit a pier and more or less knocked it. No one said anything much, just a few taunts from some of the lads, but John said quietly, 'Open your eyes, you silly donkey, and lose the stupid cap.'*

6. *I concentrated really hard next morning, and the tractor was rumbling and groaning along, and I waved to John, who was passing. Thud! I just couldn't believe it. The exact same thing happened again. This time, O'Brien strode swiftly across the yard bellowing loudly: 'Out of your wages, sonny boy, out of your wages! That'll waken you up.' The lads all had a great laugh – John too – and I wished the ground would swallow me up. For the rest of the week I was edgy. But I survived.*

7. On Monday morning, Cathal told me: 'This is the hardest job of the summer'. He was the mowing man, and his red face told of a life lived mostly outdoors. He had been working in the meadow the Saturday before. I asked him what was so hard about it.

'Real small gaps and damp ground, and if you're not careful, you could knock another pier, and get stuck in the soft fields.' He looked at me sternly as he sucked on a piece of grass. Cathal usually was an easy-going sort of a fellow, so I knew this was really serious. I was determined not to muck this up. We filled the tractors with diesel and set off.

8. We tore straight into it, and I found out just how difficult it was. There was a hair between the trailer and the pier when going into the gap, and the tractor was skidding the whole time. I got through the first day. But it was that evening when I found out what everyone thought of me. I was the last to park. The Boss was chatting to Cathal and 'Towney' was talking to Mark, who drove a similar tractor to mine, rusty and dangerous. I tuned into the chat going on around me. The Boss and Cathal were talking about how slow I was, and that I couldn't drive beside the silage harvester and fill the trailer properly. Mark and 'Towney' were sharing a laugh about how useless I was.

'Did you ever see anything like him? Waving to everyone like a schoolgirl?'

9. From this moment, I made up my mind to change. I sped up, started to fill the trailer properly, concentrated on the job to hand and quit the waving. I eyed the openings into the fields carefully, checking the soft margins before edging in. I kept at it all summer, and was soon the first to park in the evening, as I had all the jobs done. I was adjusting the trailer one night recently when I heard O'Brien's deep voice saying, 'That Paul, did you ever see such a change come over a young lad? Fine worker now!'

Word count: 973

Examiner's comment

- Well-sustained response, tracing the central character's development.
- Setting effectively established early on.
- Central character comes across as vulnerable and engaging.
- Little use of effective suggestion, e.g. in paragraph 4 ('I began to get to know the others. I met a lad named John... I hoped we'd be pals').
- Descriptive details are note-like at times. Minor characters and dialogue add authenticity.
- Ending is a little predictable ('when I heard O'Brien's deep voice saying, 'That Paul, did you ever see such a change come over a young lad? Fine worker now!')

GRADE: H3

P = 24/30

C = 22/30

L = 22/30

M = 10/10

TOTAL = 78%

CLASS/HOMEWORK EXERCISE

Based on your reading of the story, what is your impression of Paul, the central character? (Aim for at least 100 words.)

Prompt!

- Initial impression? What character traits does Paul display?
- What does his attitude to the work suggest about him?
- Does the writer contrast Paul with other characters?
- What do readers learn about him from his interaction with others?
- Has he any faults or weaknesses?
- What is revealed about him from the way he reacts in a crisis?
- How does he develop or change over the course of the story?
- Is Paul a likeable and engaging character?

CREATING CHARACTERS

* The reader has to engage and identify with the **protagonist** (the central character in the story) in order to feel interested enough to continue reading and to find out what happens to that character. Protagonists will have interesting imperfections that they fight against while striving to obtain a goal.
* The **antagonist** is the character who opposes the main character and his/her efforts to achieve his/her dream. A short story uses few characters and one of these will be central to the narrative. All major events in the plot will be important in some way to him/her.
* Characters carry your story. Without them, events have little impact. When writing short stories, aim to reveal character through action and dialogue. If possible, **avoid stereotypes**, e.g. the cruel stepmother, the brilliant detective, the drunken writer.
* Make characters different from one another by giving them particular mannerisms and voices. Characters tend to be more interesting if they have both qualities and flaws that make them vulnerable. **Memorable fictional characters stand out**, so consider giving them secrets or personality quirks.
* Stories work best when readers respond to **a character who develops** over the course of the narrative. We can relate more easily to characters if they learn something about good and evil – or love and trust.

CREATING A CHARACTER PROFILE

Name: Darren Thornton

Age: 17

Occupation: Suspended student at local community school

Appearance: Spiked black hair, sallow complexion, brown eyes, hard stare, customised school uniform with black leather jacket, steel-tipped boots, no tie

Personality: On the surface, a troublemaker, teachers see him as a threat; good sense of humour, loyal, feels less intelligent than younger brother

Hobbies: Playing darts, listening to very loud music, hanging out with friends

Ambition: To win Ireland's Darts League

Hates: PE and especially the soccer coach, Mr. Caine

CLASS/HOMEWORK EXERCISE

Create a profile for another central character, using the structure above as a guide.

A character is what he does, yes – but even more, a character is what he means to do.

Orson Scott Card

Composing

LESSON 37: FORESHADOWING IN SHORT STORIES

Learning aim: To understand how foreshadowing, tension and suspense can add interest to a short story

FORESHADOWING

> By the pricking of my thumbs,
> Something wicked this way comes
>
> From 'Macbeth' by William Shakespeare

Foreshadowing hints at where the story is going. Like a game of cat and mouse, the writer teases the reader about plot turns that may occur later in the story. This creates an atmosphere of suspense and adds dramatic tension by building up expectations. It also makes extraordinary events believable because readers have been prepared in advance for them.

As readers, we don't like to be lied to or tricked. We become frustrated and unhappy if our curiosity has been excited by foreshadowing that then leads nowhere. The exception to this is in mystery or crime writing where the author deliberately sets up false leads known as 'red herrings'. Readers of this type of genre know to expect these and enjoy trying to guess which hint is real and which is false.

We use foreshadowing in everyday conversation – for instance, to impress a friend with some juicy gossip: 'If you thought that was bad, just wait till you hear this'. Foreshadowing creates tension and suspense as the reader anxiously awaits the next stage in the plot.

USING FORESHADOWING IN A SHORT STORY

- Plant a phrase about the future early in the story.
- Introduce a subtle change in the weather or mood.
- Associate objects or settings with different emotions – happiness, sadness, danger, excitement, etc.
- Make a character observe something that could hint at a later event to come.

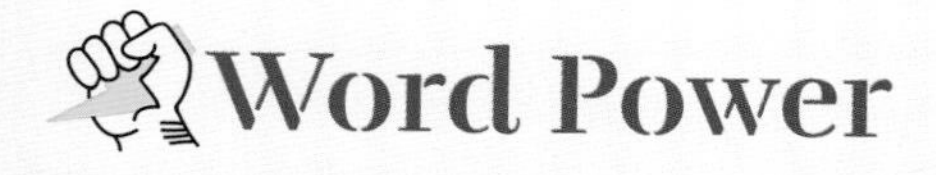

Read the short extract below from *To Kill a Mockingbird* by Harper Lee and the sample comment that follows it on the use of foreshadowing.

'I wanted you to see what real courage is, instead of getting the idea that courage is a man with a gun in his hand. It's when you know you're licked before you begin, but you begin anyway and see it through no matter what.'

This excerpt is one of the famous quotes from lawyer Atticus Finch. Atticus tells his children that courage does not come from bearing arms, but instead from trying to do something noble even when the odds are against you. This quote foreshadows the main struggle of the novel as Atticus eventually tries to defend Tom Robinson in the courtroom while knowing all along that his case has almost no hope. Atticus takes on Robinson's case not because he thinks he will win, but because he thinks it's the right thing to do.

CLASS/HOMEWORK EXERCISE

Read the following excerpt and then write a brief paragraph, (at least 50 words) commenting on the use of foreshadowing.

The car sneaked along the deserted streets, a gleaming dark predator in this cloudy, black rain-soaked winter evening. A piercing wind sounded its one desolate note as it wound between the high granite buildings. Most good souls were safely settled at their glowing firesides, but not the three grim-faced men in the car. They had business to attend to.

Sample Short Story 5

Write a short story in which a particular location or place is a significant feature.

Marking Scheme Guidelines
Reward awareness of the narrative shape of a short story (plot, character, setting, tension, foreshadowing, dialogue, etc.). The setting/location should be central to the storyline.

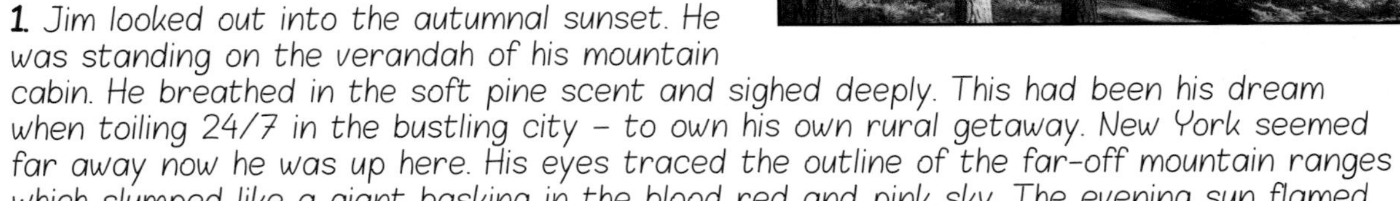

1. Jim looked out into the autumnal sunset. He was standing on the verandah of his mountain cabin. He breathed in the soft pine scent and sighed deeply. This had been his dream when toiling 24/7 in the bustling city – to own his own rural getaway. New York seemed far away now he was up here. His eyes traced the outline of the far-off mountain ranges which slumped like a giant basking in the blood red and pink sky. The evening sun flamed and was soon swallowed by the dark sleeping mountains. He felt a bitter acceptance. How ironic that it should end like this! In this cabin, above all places where everything he had ever wanted resided. He turned and went in.

2. He sat down at the head of the table, and reluctantly lowered his gaze. The seductively tender meat sat, surrounded by the sound of the cheerful chatter of the guests. The clinking cutlery added another layer of sound. The guests were clearly enjoying themselves. The red meat glistened softly on the silver serving dish. They knew! They had to know. He shook his head ruefully and got up to go to the bathroom. For a second, he leaned his perspiring head against the cold tiles. 'Mustn't panic. Got to think.' Turning on the tap, he let the warm water flow over his hands. Another scene flooded into his mind, warm and red. Jim shook his head. 'There's no evidence at all... What can they do?'

3. He splashed his face with icy water. This must have been the fifth time he had washed his hands in an hour. He gazed into the mirror. Satisfied, he smiled. All looked as it should. There was nothing in his appearance to give anything away. He remembered it perfectly. Driving up to the secluded cabin, the black trees looming ominously overhead. But he had been too excited to care. He was bringing word of his promotion... Head of Marketing. He had decided to surprise his wife and not ring ahead. He couldn't wait to see the smile on Jill's pretty face as he told her the good news. As he pulled into the driveway, he suddenly noticed that there were two cars alongside the verandah... Jill's red Polo, and another car, a low-slung black Porsche. Turning swiftly, he pulled into a forest clearing a little farther on and waited. A yawning young man with his shirt unbuttoned appeared, illuminated by the last of the day's sun. He stretched his tanned torso and called, 'Jill, darling'.

4. *Jim sat numb. Jill came out. She leaned over and kissed the young man passionately before waving him goodbye. Jim felt a dull, slow anger deep in his chest. He shook his head. They had been so happy. And now... Why had she done this to him? To them? What was she thinking of? A slow red mist filled his mind. Why had she made him do it? He stretched purposefully for the white fluffy towel monogrammed with two intertwined initials, JJ. He grimaced, but drying his hands thoroughly, he folded it neatly in two and placed it back on the heated rail. Composed, he returned to his guests.*

5. *He smiled at his manager, as he settled back at the table. 'Jim, where is that beautiful wife of yours? Have you tied her to the kitchen sink?'*

A low laugh went round the table. The manager's face glowed purple as he polished off his plate of meat and quaffed the deep red wine. 'Up north, Ger,' Jim responded, 'getting a little R & R... You know how these women are... must be pampered and cosseted.'

'Tell me about it! I think I work to employ the staff at the spa.'

Another subdued laugh reverberated and the small talk resumed.

'But, Jim, who made such a lovely meal?' asked another associate. 'It was hardly you, surely?'

'No, that's a recipe I got from my wife. She can work wonders in the kitchen. She made me do it... Anyone for dessert?'

6. *There was a spring to his step as he went back to the kitchen. He congratulated himself. Ger's question had given him the perfect opportunity to slip in his alibi. The guests had certainly enjoyed their roast. He laughed quietly. 'No evidence now'. He wasn't going to get caught. But she had been so beautiful. Long blonde hair, tanned slim body... He shook his head. What a waste!*

7. *Jim returned to the table, placing the carefully arranged slices of gateau in the centre.*

'I must say,' said Ger, 'That was the tastiest meal I've had in a long time.'

'It was a little special', replied Jim. 'Bit of a family secret, in fact... It's called Jill's Joint'. The guests raised their glasses merrily to toast the absent hostess. Jim's blue eyes glinted in the candlelight. He looked around the room and smirked – a rural getaway indeed!

Word count: 824

GRADE: H1

P = 28/30

C = 27/30

L = 27/30

M = 10/10

TOTAL = 92%

Examiner's comment

- Strong sense of time and place from the outset.
- Edgy, atmospheric scenes add drama. Red imagery is a little forced, however.
- Uneasy underlying tone throughout, e.g. paragraph 4.
- Some very good use of suggestion, e.g. paragraph 5.
- Detailed description and effective snippets of dialogue add to tension.
- Narrative focus on location right to the final line.

CLASS/HOMEWORK EXERCISE

Deconstruct the above story using the outline guide below to help you. Respond briefly to each question, using suitable reference and quotation.

Paragraph 1: Introduction
Where and when is the story set? Who is the main character? Is he content or uneasy? Is the mood relaxed? How has the author used foreshadowing in his descriptions of the setting to make the reader curious?

Paragraph 2: Foreshadowing
What item is vividly described? Why do you think the writer makes the reader focus on this object?

Paragraphs 3/4: Flashback
How does the flashback provide a motive for the central character?

Paragraph 5: Ambiguity
Now that the tension is nearing its height, what phrases have more than one meaning? Is there an echo from paragraph 4? What effect does this have on the reader?

Paragraphs 5: Foreshadowing
What items are vividly described? Why is the writer making the reader focus on this item?

Paragraph 6: Flashback
Who might readers have sympathy with at this stage? Why?

Paragraph 7: Resolution
What effect does the description of the cut gateau have on the reader?

Has the writer provided a satisfactory pay-off for the reader after the hints that were placed throughout the story? Comment on the ending.

Tension and **suspense** provide the electric current that runs through a story, keeping the reader engaged and turning the page. Tension happens in a story when the reader cares about the characters. It usually occurs as a result of the basic conflict in a story. The rising action (the obstacles the character has to overcome to achieve his/her goal) complicates the plot as the story rises to its climax. The interaction of the opposing narrative forces creates feelings of uneasiness.

Suspense and tension are different concepts, although they often work together in a story. Suspense is the emotion generated by questions in the plot such as: 'Who did it?' and 'Why?' Tension is the strain of emotions you experience when a character you care about is in jeopardy.

Together, tension and suspense involve the reader, resulting in a satisfying resolution of the conflict.

Tension and Suspense in Sample Short Story 5

* There is a tense, uncomfortable move at the start of the story. It arises from the conflict affecting the central character.
Jim is hurt when his wife, Jill, cheats on him.

* **Likeable characters** make the reader care about what happens to them.
Jim is a young hard-working man rushing home to share the good news of his promotion with his beautiful wife. The reader will wonder about how Jim will react to his wife's infidelity.

* The writer keeps **raising the stakes**.
Jim loses his cool and repeatedly washes his hands.

* At times, there is **ebb and flow** in the tension. Some sentences relax the mood.
'Composed, he returned to his guests.'

* **Short sentences** convey tension.
Jim sat numb. Jill came out.

* **Dialogue** (direct and interior) can increase tension.
'Jim, where is that beautiful wife of yours? Have you tied her to the kitchen sink?'

Direct dialogue challenges the character. Will he be discovered?
'Mustn't panic. Got to think.'

Indirect dialogue allows the reader to share the character's anxiety.

Suspense is created in a story by making the reader uneasy. It can be a pleasurable anticipation as the reader waits 'on-edge', in a state of apprehension or even dread of what will happen next. Suspense occurs between the promise of something dreadful or exciting and its arrival.
'They knew! They had to know.'

Foreshadowing is one technique that can be used effectively. The movie director Alfred Hitchcock, the master of suspense, withheld information from the main characters. He often placed audiences with a superior perspective by allowing them to know what is going to happen while being in a powerless position to prevent it.
'Now, let us take a suspense situation. The bomb is underneath the table and the public knows it, probably because they have seen the anarchist place it there. The public is aware the bomb is going to explode at one o'clock and there is a clock in the decor. The public can see that it is a quarter to one. In these conditions, the same innocuous conversation becomes fascinating because the public is participating in the scene. The audience is longing to warn the characters on the screen: "You shouldn't be talking about such trivial matters. There is a bomb beneath you and it is about to explode!"'

This is very similar to the experience of small children at a pantomime warning the unsuspecting hero about the villain: 'He's behind you!'

CLASS/HOMEWORK EXERCISE

Imagine that you are planning to write a short story in which a mystery or crime is solved. Make out a plan for the story (at least six points) outlining the plot and including some of the techniques you would use to increase the tension and suspense.

This suspense is terrible, I hope it will last.

Oscar Wilde

Composing

LESSON 38: POINT OF VIEW IN SHORT STORIES

Learning aim: To understand narrative point of view and to use dialogue effectively

POINT OF VIEW

Literature provides a window through which readers look at the world.

Stories show us both the good and the bad in human nature. A story can be a way of making sense of the world, or even making something beautiful and entertaining out of what might otherwise just be painful. We tell stories for many reasons – to entertain and illuminate – and to prevent us making the same mistakes.

Point of view is the perspective from which a story is told – the narrator's position in relation to the narrative. There are several narrative viewpoints used in popular fiction. The story may be told by the central character so the reader sees the action through the character's eyes. This is **First Person Point of View** and features the following pronouns: I, me, mine, our, we, us, etc. The reader usually relates to this character and will have empathy for the character's views and feelings.

'The wind stung my cheeks as I felt the rush of speed. The bright red Porsche clung to the curves of the Californian cliff side. I felt the throb of the engine as it purred smoothly eating up the road. Up here I could breathe. Up here, I felt the adrenalin rush as the country whipped by.'

In this extract from Sample Short Story 3, the reader is placed in the car alongside the driver. We share the same experiences and feel the same sensations.

In contrast, stories written from a **Third Person Point of View** describe what is happening to the characters in the story, referring to them by their names or using pronouns: he she, it, they, them, etc. The third person narrator is usually not a character in the story.

Third person narratives are one of the most commonly used narrative modes. The narrator may be **omniscient** (all-knowing), able to see into the thoughts and feelings of all the characters, almost like a god-like figure looking down on the action or sometimes **limited** – knowing the thoughts and feelings of only one character.

In the extract below, the reader views the action from the character's (Annie's) point of view, but the author directly describes the character: 'A faint pink stain crept up Annie's cheek'. The omniscient narrative voice invites readers to relate to the central character.

The lights froze in their strobe-like movement and shone solely on him. His scarlet shoes matched the tie of his suit and the mask on his face. His long black curly hair hung in masses around the mask. Even the snarling face of Lucifer he wore could not obliterate his beauty, an Adonis amid a crowd of satyrs. A faint pink stain crept up Annie's cheek. He had caught her staring. Embarrassed she turned to lean on the safety of the bar.

CLASS/HOMEWORK EXERCISE

Read the following three passages and identify the point of view used. Comment on its effect. (The first one is already done for you.)

1. 'Regis touched his face and felt swollen flesh on the side of his mouth. It was funny but it didn't hurt at all. Then he realised the swollen flesh was a leech growing fat as it sucked his lips. It was practically in his mouth.'

From **Jurassic Park** by Michael Crichton

Composing

Sample Answer

The point of view used here is **Third Person**. The reader sees the action through Regis's eyes only. This limited view adds to the horror of the situation because the reader can only feel what Regis is experiencing.

2. 'It was times like these when I thought my father, who hated guns and had never been to any wars, was the bravest man who ever lived.'

From *To Kill a Mockingbird* by Harper Lee

3. 'Margaret, the eldest of the four, was sixteen, and very pretty, being plump and fair, with large eyes, plenty of soft brown hair, a sweet mouth, and white hands, of which she was rather vain. Fifteen-year-old Jo was very tall, thin, and brown, and reminded one of a colt... Elizabeth, or Beth, as everyone called her, was a rosy, smooth-haired, bright-eyed girl of thirteen, with a shy manner, a timid voice, and a peaceful expression, which was seldom disturbed.'

From *Little Women* by Louisa May Alcott

Sample Short Story 6

Write a short story that involves a transformation in the circumstances of one or more of the central characters.

Marking Scheme Guidelines

Reward awareness of the narrative shape of a story (plot, character, setting, dialogue, point of view, etc.). Interpret the term 'transformation' liberally. However, the story should include some element of change that affects the lives of one or more characters.

1. It's the stuff we don't say. The pauses. The squeeze of the arm. The Irish drizzle soaked the windscreen. No wipers could clear it. The grey road stretched endlessly in front of me. Speed signs blurred by, 80km, 100km. Large transport lorries threw sheets of blinding water against the window. I had to keep going. I checked the clock... Two more hours. Sodden, green, rain-soaked fields merged into one long border as the car slowly ate up the road. I turned off the radio. It jarred. The window wipers clicked mechanically, steadily marking the ebbing day. I checked the petrol gauge – nearly empty. There should be a station somewhere near here. I peered out at the downpour. Through the grey mists, four huddled statues appear at the turn for Lake Derravaragh. Mum had called us after them, Aodh, Fionnuala, Fiachra and Conn.

2. We used to swim in cold Lake Derravaragh and have mad picnics on the lakeshore. Mum with her Primus stove in the old biscuit tin box would fry golden sausages or heat stew in the big aluminium pot. Her "Children of Lir" would come running up the grass, blue-grey with cold, goose bumps on goose bumps after a swim in the icy lake. What memories – jumping down on the rough towels lying on the ground, laughing and joking, mouths full. Moments that merit a frame, but that was how it always was, so we didn't need to take any pictures. The red rosehips glinted in the autumnal sunshine and Mum's chuckles filled the air as she enveloped us into a giant 'big squeeze', her blonde curls bobbing.

3. The distant pictures of carefree days flashed through my mind, autumnal walks in Ravensdale Park, the dry bracken crunching under our feet, my brothers hurrying back

Composing

to show what treasures they had found, unaware that the greatest treasure was just us all being together, happy and well. Cottage bread toasted by the open fire at home, golden butter sliding over its warm surface... Memories, enveloped in the security of family.

4. *I drive through one midland town after another, all the same, rain-soaked, deserted. Finally, I reach the big, grey granite building, swing into the familiar car park, and join the others, walking the same corridors, the two flights of stairs, and there she is. A stark contrast to the banal journey regularly made. Everything is new to her. The poet Kavanagh would be proud. She does see the extraordinary in the ordinary. 'Well, it all seems new to me!' The pity of it is that she won't remember saying that in twenty minutes' time. A frail papery hand tips my arm.*

5. *He is stroking her arm mechanically. Dad was her first boyfriend. They used to date in secret. She gazes up quizzically, unsure, half-smiling. He looks over her head, no longer explaining anything. What is there to say? She points towards the same unread magazine she has shown us the last three times we have come. 'Look at what I have for you. I never miss it every Friday... Would you like to see?' I take it from her and try to smile. Dad stands up, his back to us, clearing his throat with that rasping dry cough. She pulls distractedly at the various tubes that entrap her, under as cruel a spell as Aoife had cast on her stepchildren all those long ages ago.*

6. *A young, fresh-faced nurse bustles in, clattering cups and saucers on a squeaky trolley. 'Tea, Mrs Maguire?' she inquires.*

Mum nods. Not quite sure. 'No mushrooms, I can't eat them, especially the tinned ones. Sure they don't taste like mushrooms at all... It's a good enough place, although the guests don't dress up like they used to.' The nurse is on a schedule and quickly ushers us out. Our time is up. 'So good of you to come. She is quite happy, you know.'

We didn't. Mum waves an unquestioning goodbye.

7. *We stand huddled together in the car park, holding each other tight; silhouetted, fowl-like 'Children of Lir'. This time the spell can't be broken. The waiting won't be magical. It can never be how it always was.*

It's the stuff we don't say. The pauses... The squeeze of the arm.

Word count: 712

Examiner's comment

- Well-paced short story, exploring transformed lives.
- Strong first person viewpoint engages readers.
- Setting is effectively evoked.
- Contrasting time-frames and moods work well.
- Some very good use of suggestion, e.g. in paragraph 5 ('She gazes up quizzically, unsure, half-smiling. He looks over her head, no longer explaining anything. What is there to say?').
- Detailed description and dialogue add authenticity.
- Narrative is rounded off effectively, echoing the opening ('Children of Lir').

GRADE: H1

P = 30/30

C = 27/30

L = 28/30

M = 10/10

TOTAL = 95%

CLASS/HOMEWORK EXERCISES

1. The writer has chosen a first person point of view for this story. Write a paragraph commenting on its effectiveness in communicating the narrative.

2. Rewrite the opening paragraph using a different point of view. Do not use 'I'.

Word Power

Dialogue is used in a story to:

* set the scene * advance action * give insight into character/s * create mood/atmosphere * foreshadow.

Dialogue does not always have to be grammatically correct, but it must be realistic enough to engage readers.

THE RULES OF DIALOGUE

1. Use a capital letter. Put inverted commas around what the character says. Place commas, full stops, exclamation and question marks that refer to the direct speech inside the inverted commas.

INCORRECT
'See you soon', said Mary.

CORRECT
'See you soon,' said Mary.

2. Use a new line for each speaker. The new line signals another person is speaking.

INCORRECT
'I wish the Leaving Cert was over,' Deirdre sighed. 'Don't wish your life away,' Dad replied.

CORRECT
'I wish the Leaving Cert. was over,' Deirdre sighed.
'Don't wish your life away,' Dad replied.

3. Break up a long line of dialogue into two parts so the reader can picture who is speaking.

INCORRECT
'I just don't believe I've failed. I studied and studied, but I just went blank… I guess I'm going to have to re-sit,' said Niall.

CORRECT
'I just don't believe I've failed,' said Niall. 'I studied and studied, but I just went blank… I guess I'm going to have to re-sit.'

4. Avoid too many dialogue verbs/tags as they can overshadow the actual words being spoken. If only two people are speaking, once you have established who they are, you can drop the dialogue verbs/tags altogether. Keep it simple.

INCORRECT
'You have broken my heart,' she sobbed.
'Don't blame me!' he muttered.
'You cheated on me!' she screamed.
'I don't know – it just happened,' he mumbled.
'OOOH!' she cried.

CORRECT
'You have broken my heart,' she sobbed.
'Don't blame me,' he said.
'You cheated on me!'
'I don't know – it just happened.'
'OOOH!'

5. Use action to show who is speaking. Whoever is given action afterwards is the speaker.

INCORRECT
Sophie walked towards him. 'I really do love you, y'know.' Terry winced.

CORRECT
Sophie walked towards him. 'I really do love you, y'know.' She held out her arms. Terry winced.

N.B. Some writers dispense with the rules for dialogue, often just using a new line with no punctuation marks to indicate speech. For the Leaving Certificate examination, however, it's best to use the formal rules for dialogue.

CLASS/HOMEWORK EXERCISE

Rewrite the following passage using the guidelines for dialogue above to make the story clearer for the reader.

Do you see that? She dumped a fresh pot of coffee in the sink. Yeah, I confirmed pointing to the steam. Lady in booth 51 thinks the coffee's too cold. Lynda grimaced stomping her foot. Sharing her frustration, I offered my advice. Maybe you should spill it on her, so she'll know how hot it is. We giggled secretly, wishing it was an option. I watched Lynda take the rest of the lady's order as I coiled myself in the corner of booth 61, across from 51, my styrofoam cup of coffee blowing fragrant steam at my face. OOPS! cried Lynda as the hot brown liquid trickled onto the lady's arm. Lynda glanced over and winked. I couldn't believe she'd done it. I never would have had the nerve. Lynda dabbed energetically with her napkin as the lady curled her thin lips.

An example of dialogue falling short!

Composing

LESSON 39: ENDING SHORT STORIES

Learning aim: To conclude a short story successfully and to explore aesthetic writing

THE END

> People die, love dies, but life does not die, and so long as people live, stories must have life at the end.
>
> John O'Hara

There is no single right or wrong approach to ending a short story, but most writers usually know how the narrative will end before they begin, and so they can focus on the **resolution** as they are writing.

Concluding a story must leave the reader satisfied that the ending is credible within the 'world' of the story and it must be true to its characters. A successful conclusion solves the central conflict. This can be done **happily** or **unhappily**.

The writer can provide a **twist in the tale** (the reader does not anticipate what happens, but the event must not be out of place in the story).

The ending can be **closed**, so that nothing more can happen, or **open** with just a suggestion of what the character will do next.

Readers will expect the conclusion to **tie up the loose ends** and answer any questions that have arisen over the course of the story. What was promised must be delivered.

HOW TO END A STORY SUCCESSFULLY

- Resolve the main conflict in a credible way.
- Look to the beginning of the story to find the end. Circular motion works well for the reader because there is a sense of finality.
- End loosely, leaving something for the reader to conclude. Endings should be poignant and thought-provoking. If the conclusion is too neat, it trivialises the story.
- A cliff-hanger leaves the reader to decide what was going to happen next.
- The ending should make an impact – something should have been learned about human nature or the human condition without being preachy, moralistic or didactic.

> People think that stories are shaped by people. In fact it's the other way round.
>
> Terry Pratchett

ENDINGS TO AVOID

Respect your reader by avoiding unconvincing endings, such as:

- And then I woke up.
- I caught up with him and shot him.
- It was a man in a mask all along.
- It was my evil twin, we were separated at birth.
- You see, I'm really a dog/demon/alien.

Sample Short Story 7

Write a short story in which there is a supernatural or surreal element.

Marking Scheme Guidelines
Reward awareness of the narrative shape of a short story (plot, character, setting, conflict, dialogue, etc.). The supernatural/ surreal element should play a significant part in the story.

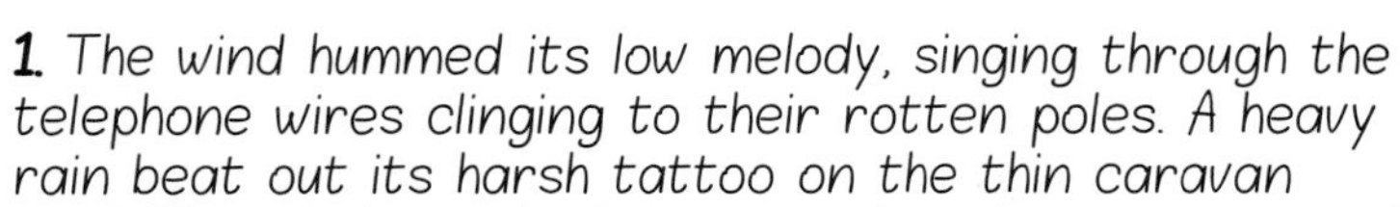

1. The wind hummed its low melody, singing through the telephone wires clinging to their rotten poles. A heavy rain beat out its harsh tattoo on the thin caravan roof. The wind-wracked caravan played an accompanying rocking descant. Vicious waves snarled against the beach, hungrily scavenging its detritus. Flashes of lightning illuminated the pretty pink and green shoe that was quickly gulped by the ravenous sea. Another flash shone on the headline of the old newspaper, 'Freak wave swept eleven-year old Betty Carvill to certain death!' I peered out into the storm. Joe shouldn't be long now; he had just gone out to check the gas tank.

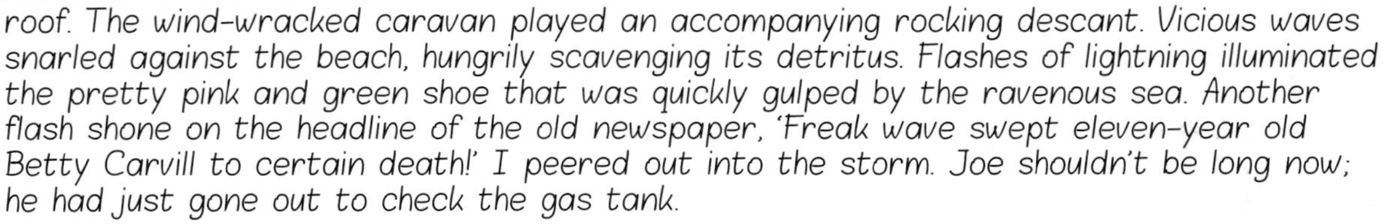

2. A cold gust of wind swept round the old caravan as the door burst open. A tall black shadow stood silhouetted. 'Well, that wind would nip the ears off you, so it would.' I smiled. 'Ah, Joe!' His eyes were dancing with excitement. 'C'mon Helen. Let's go up the cliffs and see nature's show. The waves should be at least ten metres, maybe fifteen! Get your coat!' Well why not? The full moon shone its spotlight on the shore. Let the show begin. Pulling my anorak on, I slammed the door shut and began to scramble after him. 'Hold on!'

3. My words were whipped away by the merciless wind. Suddenly Joe's large hand gripped me, helping me keep my balance while we climbed to the cliff top.

'There, little sis, wasn't it worth it?'

Nature really had pulled out all the stops this time. Huge black waves, ruffled with dainty salt spray crashed against the rocks below. A long glistening roadway was thrown onto the restless sea by the pale moon. Joe and I danced with joy. The salty shower of spray rose and the ground laughed and trembled. I felt alive and free. I whirled and whirled, no longer feeling the ground beneath me. A strange calm descended on me and I spiralled through the turbulent air. Suddenly, a huge wave enveloped me and I gasped for air as I sank into its blackness.

4. Choking and spluttering, I tried to open my heavy lids. Large, grey stone walls shone with embedded barnacles. Dark green moss carpeted the floor. I put my hand to my throbbing head and almost slid off the stone slab. I looked at my legs, ink bruises on white parchment. I slid back into darkness. Gentle singing woke me. The swish of the bladder wrack stopped and two large green eyes peered into mine.

'Hi there, silly-billy! Are you feeling any better?'

'I think so. Who are you?'

Soft tinkling laughter followed.

'I don't know. I dropped from the sky like you. I call myself Coralie... But who are you?'

'I am... I don't know!'

'I knew you were silly. I'll call you Mossi.'

'But I have to get back – I need to get back!'

'To where?'

'I'm not sure... I don't know.'

'There's no way out.'

'What do you mean?'

'I've been here a very long time... You better have something to eat.'

5. Coralie handed me the largest shell I had ever seen, full of delicious fish morsels garnished with fronds of seaweed. It was good to eat. I felt satisfied. The cave was shining, iridescent with silver, red, green and coral. Coralie sighed happily. In the pool on the far left, a deep surge of water... but as the water ebbed I suddenly knew, 'Tides!'

'Coralie, if we watch the pool carefully, we can determine when the tides come in and go out.' But she wasn't interested. It was as though she didn't hear me.

I slipped into the pool and felt the pull of the water. I dived and saw a light in the distance.

'I am going to have a go. I will get help.'

But Coralie was singing gently to herself, happily arranging her sea ornaments.

6. I took a deep breath and launched myself into the whirling water. The surge carried me and I felt the pain in my lungs as I tried to hold my breath. Suddenly I was going up, the light was becoming brighter. I struck out with my remaining strength and a huge wave deposited me on the warm sand.

7. 'She's over here!' A flurry of running feet and then two strong arms lifted me.

'Thank God, little sis, thought you were gone like Mam and Dad.'

I leaned against his strong body and opened my eyes.

'Coralie is down there. We have to get her... Please!'

'Helen, stop. Oh, she is delirious. It's all right, Helen!'

'But I am telling you – she lives down there.'

Examiner's comment

- Sustained dream-like atmosphere throughout.
- Surreal mood established in the exaggerated setting, e.g. paragraph 1.
- Central character comes across as childlike and disoriented.
- Minor characters have a distant other-worldly presence.
- Effective use of ominous details, e.g. the news headline.
- Some less convincing moments,– e.g. paragraph 5. ('I dived and saw a light in the distance, 'I am going to have a go. I will get help').
- Unnerving sense of nature as being both beautiful and destructive.
- Precise description, e.g. paragraph. 4 – 'Large, grey stone walls shone with embedded barnacles. Dark green moss carpeted the floor'– creates a vivid nightmarish setting.
- Open ending leaves readers wondering.

'Don't worry, Joe, we'll look after Helen. She's had a terrible experience. It will take time to recover,' soothed a voice.

'But Coralie... What about her?'

A sharp needle prick heralded a soft peaceful darkness.

The ambulance door slammed shut.

Word count: 812

GRADE: H2

P = 27/30

C = 24/30

L = 27/30

M = 10/10

TOTAL = 88%

CLASS/HOMEWORK EXERCISES

1. Write a paragraph (at least 100 words) commenting on the effectiveness of the ending of this story. In your opinion, did it end happily, unhappily, closed, open or with a twist in the tale? Was the conclusion satisfactory – considering the setting and characters in the story?

2. Below are two alternative endings to the story. Comment on the effectiveness of each one and explain which, if any, would provide a credible conclusion.

Ending 1
Joe settled happily beside his sister in the ambulance. She would be safe now. She was going to get the best medical treatment possible. He would see to that. He knew she was going to make a real recovery and would soon forget all this ridiculous Coralie nonsense.

Ending 2
I struck out with my remaining strength and a huge wave deposited me back in the cave.

'See, didn't I tell you! Now you know you can't ever escape.' Coralie chuckled quietly to herself. 'Silly Mossi… I can't leave you alone for a moment.' I cradled my head in my hands. The tears flowed.

It ain't whatcha write, it's the way atcha write it.

Jack Kerouac

Word Power

Aesthetic language is artistic and carefully crafted – and often has poetic features that appeal to the reader's appreciation of beauty.

Unlike mere functional writing, **aesthetic language usually excites our imaginations**. Of course, every kind of good appropriate writing can have aesthetic qualities. Fiction writers frequently use the techniques of alliteration, assonance, personification, onomatopoeia, repetition, etc. However, while narrative writing incorporates the use of aesthetic language, it must be used sparingly to be truly effective.

In short story 7, the opening description of the stormy night is an exercise in the use of aesthetic language. The energy of the language makes the setting come to life and heightens the **dramatic impact**.

Onomatopoeia is used to describe the wind, ('hummed', 'singing').

Other elements of the landscape are **personified**: telephone wires are 'clinging'; the rain 'beat out its harsh tattoo' and 'Vicious waves snarled'.

Dynamic verbs convey the vitality of the scene: 'whirled and whirled', 'spiralled'.

Vibrant colours portray the undersea cave: 'shining iridescent with silver, red, green and coral'.

CLASS/HOMEWORK EXERCISE

Write an opening paragraph (at least 100 words) for a science fiction or mystery story incorporating some features of aesthetic narrative to convey the setting, mood or character.

Stories make us more alive, more human, more courageous, more loving.

Madeleine L'Engle

LESSON 40: GRAMMAR AND SPELLING REVISION

Learning aim: To revise essential grammar and spelling

MECHANICS

Marks awarded for Accuracy of Mechanics (M) refer to spelling and grammar, appropriate to the register. Marks for M are essentially independent of Purpose (P), Coherence (C) and Language (L) marks.

Correct grammar is essential for clarity and understanding. It can be defined in various ways:

- The structure and analysis of sentences. This includes the study of syntax (word order) and **morphology** (word formation).
- The **basic language** rules about usage of Standard English that is widely regarded as correct and acceptable.

WORD CLASS (Parts of Speech)	FUNCTION	EXAMPLE
Nouns	'naming words'	Limerick, lunch, happiness, group
Verbs	'doing words'	imagine, sing, comprehend, defy
Adjectives	'describing words'	enormous, critical, wry, positive
Adverbs	mainly describe verbs	incredibly, most, really, quite
Pronouns	take the place of nouns	I, she, him, me, their, it, our
Connectives	'joining words'	and, or, if, but, so, because, yet
Prepositions	provide information about time and place	since, before, until, through, next to

SOME COMMONLY MISUSED WORDS

English is full of words that sound alike and are spelled similarly but have a different meaning and are easily confused. A computer spell-checker will not highlight a word that is spelled correctly but used incorrectly, so if you are uncertain about the correct spelling of a particular word, check it in a dictionary.

Some commonly confused words are listed below.

Accept: verb meaning to 'agree' or to 'receive' something.
Except: preposition meaning 'with the exclusion of'.

E.g. I would like you to accept this small gift.
All his friends came to the party except for Kate who was in hospital.

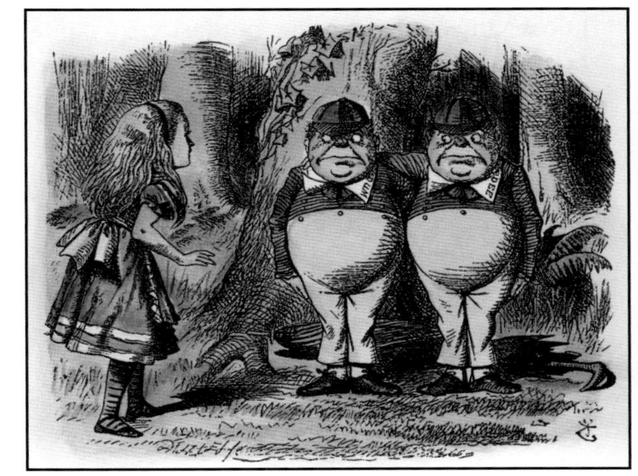

The infamous Tweedledum and Tweedledee from Lewis Carroll's
'Through the Looking Glass and What Alice Found There'

Composing

Advice: noun meaning an opinion or recommendation offered as guidance.
Advise: verb meaning to 'counsel' or make a suggestion.

E.g. Declan gave me some good advice about the problem of noisy neighbours.
I also asked Ciara to advise me about my noisy neighbours.

Affect: verb meaning to 'influence'.
Effect: noun meaning the 'result of an action'.

E.g. Poor grammar may affect your marks.
Poor grammar had a huge effect on his results.

Allowed: past participle of the verb 'to allow' and means 'permitted'.
Aloud: adjective, meaning 'out loud'.

E.g. The children are not allowed to go to the cinema this evening.
John was asked to read the poem aloud.

Have: verb that usually follows other 'doing words'.
Of: preposition used in phrases.

E.g. Nicky could probably have played for Leinster.
Colin watches lots of sport on TV.

Incredible: so implausible as to elicit disbelief/astonishment.
Incredulous: sceptical or disbelieving.

E.g. The witness's evidence was utterly incredible.
When I first heard the rumours, I was utterly incredulous.

Its: meaning 'belong to it'.
It's: short form of 'it is'.

E.g. Sara's kitten keeps licking its paw.
It's time for our class to go to the gym.

Less: usually describes single items.
Fewer: refers to people or things in the plural.

E.g. My friend is spending less time with me these days.
We would have fewer arguments if I wasn't so pedantic.

Loose: adjective meaning 'not fastened, contained or restrained'.
Lose: verb, has many meanings such as to 'not win' or to 'mislay'.

E.g. That roof tile is loose and might fall at any minute.
Let's hope we don't lose the match on Saturday.

Passed: past tense of the verb to 'pass'.
Past: the time before the present, no longer current.

E.g. Ben passed the ball to the striker.
Lucy hoped that the unfortunate incident was now firmly in the past.

Practise: verb meaning to 'prepare'.
Practice: noun meaning 'preparation'.

E.g. Emily practised her lines for the school play.
It takes a lot of practice to become fluent in Irish.

Principal: adjective or noun, meaning most important or chief.
Principle: noun meaning 'fundamental idea or belief'.

E.g. Paris is France's principal city.
The principle of free speech should never be taken for granted.
The children were apprehensive about meeting the new school principal.

Quite: adverb, means 'not completely'.
Quiet: adjective, means 'not noisy'.

E.g. The children are exceptionally quiet today... Spooky or what?
I've been quite busy all day. I hope things ease up soon.

Stationary: adjective, meaning 'not moving'.
Stationery: noun, meaning 'office supplies'.

E.g. The bus remained stationary until the traffic lights turned green.
Our school secretary is in charge of ordering stationery.

Uninterested: means 'to find something boring'.
Disinterested: means 'impartial'.

E.g. I was completely uninterested in that dreary documentary.
The judge is personally disinterested in the outcome of the case.

Whether: used in indirect questions to introduce one alternative.
Weather: noun meaning the 'state of the atmosphere.'

E.g. I'm not sure whether she is from Balbriggan or from Blackrock.
I am certain that the weather is going to be fantastic tomorrow.

Your: pronoun meaning 'belonging to you'.
You're: the contracted form of 'you are'.

E.g. Your dad's van is blocking our drive.
It looks like you're going nowhere.

USE THE RIGHT PHRASE!

- **'A lot'** means 'many' and should be written as two separate words.
- **'As well'** is also written as two words.
- **'May be'** usually means **'might be'** whereas 'maybe' means 'perhaps'.
- **'No one'** is two words while **'nobody'** is one word.
- **'Thank you'** is always written as two words.

IMPROVING LEAVING CERTIFICATE ANSWERS

Your written responses always need to be **carefully planned** and organised. Ordering your points should also take place at the planning stage. You can then use paragraphs to take the examiner step-by-step through each section.

PARAGRAPH ALERT!

A paragraph is a section of text, usually consisting of several sentences, which addresses a particular topic or aspect of a subject. A paragraph may occasionally be one sentence (or even one word) to make a particular effect.

Why use paragraphs?

Paragraphs break up long texts and give **structure** to a piece of writing. They help to organise your thoughts and clarify your ideas.

Every paragraph should discuss just **one main idea**, so that the examiner is able to identify what it is about. New paragraphs indicate a change of focus.

Paragraphs often start with a topic sentence – an introductory key statement which is expanded in the rest of the paragraph. The **topic sentence** acts as a 'signpost' for the rest of the answer and should also relate back to the exam question.

CLASS/HOMEWORK EXERCISE

Identify the topic sentence in each of the following paragraphs and comment briefly on how the central idea is developed within the rest of the paragraph.
(The first one is done for you.)

1. More emphasis on truth is also needed in the business world. Big businesses employ smart lawyers to find loopholes in the law to avoid paying taxes, to find ways around planning restrictions, to amalgamate, to liquidate. Advertising agencies are employed to fill the potential consumer with fear or impossible dreams in order to convince them to buy. The truth is often, unlike the profits, in short supply. 'You will get bad skin if you do not use our product,' they threaten. 'You will always look young if you use our product,' they promise.

Answer: **The topic sentence is 'More emphasis on truth is also needed in the business world.'**
This is an illustrative paragraph that gives examples of the lack of honesty in big business, either by employing 'smart lawyers' or fooling the customer with threats or flattery.

2. Medical research has significantly lengthened our lives with new medicines and treatments such as laser surgery. Early diagnosis is now the key to prevention a swell as cure. A vaccine is now available to protect against cervical cancer. We are waiting on the day when cancer is also a curable disease like polio and leprosy. The fight against AIDS is progressing and we are now able to offer laser eye treatment to people to restore twenty/twenty vision. There is no limit to the possibilities for science and technology in the future.

3. In the dark arena a flash of silver gleams as the discordant tuning of the orchestra saws monotonously. The sound engineers with their familiar 'testing one tew, one tew' finish checking the stage microphones. The percussion players march on stage. A crystal clear 'A' soars from the oboe and we are in tune. Applause ripples from the audience as the conductor enters. A moment's pause as the slim white baton rises, the audience holds its breath and the warm opening notes of 'The Mikado Overture' transport all to the world of Japan. This is the magic of live performance.

How long should a paragraph be?

There is no absolute rule, but as a general guide, it will usually take at least three or four sentences to make a point and develop it with reference or commentary. The main aim is to use paragraphs appropriately – and this will depend on the actual question, the time available, and, of course, the language genre.

When do I start a new paragraph?

Start a **new paragraph for each new point or stage** in your writing. Be aware of the main idea being expressed in your paragraph and how clear it is for your reader.

In all hand-written answers, either indent or skip a line for new paragraphs.

Paragraph problems

1. Lack of focus or development.
2. Poorly organised, hard to follow.
3. No relation or links between individual sentences.
4. Too many ideas in one paragraph.
5. Too general and lacking specific detail.

CLASS/HOMEWORK EXERCISE

Identify the topic sentence in each of the following paragraphs and comment briefly on how successful each paragraph is.

1. The crowd split like the Red Sea, one half to the smoking area, the other half to the bar. All around us conversations rose, like the buzzing of an angry swarm of bees, as the merits and demerits of the first half were hotly debated. The pride of a city was at stake. We didn't have much else, up our area. But we knew how to support our team. Go lads – make us proud. As the teams re-emerged on the screen, red faces became almost black as blood pressure soared. Kerry got the better start, but Galway hung on. As the clock wound down, people began to whisper about penalties and away goals. The air was thick with tension.

2. I like to consider myself as an actor. I enjoy becoming someone else for a few hours and looking at life from a different perspective. We all remember our experiences at 'acting' in primary school, whether you were the one who starred in the Nativity play as you proclaimed, 'Follow the star to Bethlehem' or you were the one who refused to wear tights to play the part of Rat in *The Pied Piper of Hamlin*, you never forget the experience. You have lived in a heightened place. My speech and drama teacher was Mrs. Molloy and I will have to confess that at the beginning it was the large bar of Cadbury's Milk Chocolate I got when I paid the fee and the comics on her sofa which encouraged me to go. But 'education is not about filling a bucket, it's about lighting a fire' and when she brought us to The Gate Theatre to see *A Christmas Carol*, I was hooked. The colour, the sounds, but most of all the words transported me to another place another time as I lived intensely in Dickens's London, terrified of the miserly Scrooge, delighted with Tiny Tim. The real experience of performance can change lives.

> I hate writing, I love having written.
>
> Dorothy Parker

CLASS/HOMEWORK REVISION EXERCISES

1. Find the five spelling errors in this passage and correct them:

Jenny is my best freind, but she can be quiet wierd at times. In fact, she's begining to get on my nerves about all the celibritys she keeps mentioning.

2. Underline the correct option in the following passage:

I really want my sister to get her driving license/licence so that she can drive me to football practise/practice every second night. I've adviced/advised her to practise/practice as much as possible.

3. Rewrite the following sentences so that they make sense:

(a) Did you notice those monkeys over their at the cars?
(b) They've actually taken there windscreen wipers.
(c) There so cute.
(d) I think their now hiding over they're.

4. Underline the correct word in the following:

(a) The Irish Finance Ministers'/Minister's spokesperson was not impressed.
(b) Jim threw the men's/mens' shoes into the bin.
(c) The student's/students' noses all turned blue in the cold.
(d) The baby's/babys' howling could be heard three streets away.

5. Rewrite the following sentences so that they make sense:

(a) Who's/Whose going to the party?
(b) Who's/Whose bag is this?

6. Rewrite each of these sentences correctly:

(a) Such inmature and inconsiderate behaviour fills me with unbelief.
(b) Misfortunately, we were inaware that the ticket was unvalid.
(c) It was disbelievable that the writing was so unlegible.
(d) Some of the rules were completely unrelevant.

7. Underline the correct option in the following passage:

(a) How does eating too much chocolate effect/affect your blood sugar?
(b) We should of/have brought hats and umbrellas with us.
(c) The principle/principal ingredients of bread are flour, water and yeast.
(d) Deirdre will not be able to accept/except the new job offer.

8. Rewrite, choosing the correct options:

The button on my sleeve is (loose, lose) and if I (loose, lose) that button, I am in serious trouble.

9. Rewrite the following, correcting all errors:

the great american writer mark twain once said when i was a boy of 14 my father was so ignorant I could hardly stand to have the old man around but when i got to be 21 I was astonished at how much the old man had learned in seven years

10. Rewrite the following, adding all necessary punctuation and speech marks:

Have you found the advanced philosophy course interesting and fruitful, my dear he asked. His tone indicated that he was a little fearful she might say no. He peered over his half-glasses. Oh Dr Morgan how could it be otherwise, when we have the benefit of such an amazingly awesome mind like yours applying itself to the greatest, most profound, issues of the human condition? Yes indeed I'm glad you noticed that he intoned. Not to mention that you're such a totally charming gentleman. Ciara batted her eyes at him, sending a shower of mascara down his eye-catching lurid pink tie. Charming is good… Keep talking Morgan mumbled as he stuffed one of the ridiculously small sandwiches into his mouth

(Answers on page 152)

Candidates who displayed a capacity to communicate fluently and effectively were rewarded. However, the management and control of language continues to pose problems for some candidates and, in particular, poor attention to the formal aspects of language, such as spelling, grammar and punctuation, was noted in some responses.

Chief Examiner's Report (www.examinations.ie)

ANSWERS TO REVISION EXERCISES

1. friend, quite, weird, beginning, celebrities
2. I really want my sister to get her driving license/licence so that she can drive me to football practise/practice every second night. I've adviced/advised her to practice/practise as much as possible.
3. (a) Did you notice those monkeys over there at the cars?

   (b) They've actually taken their windscreen wipers.

   (c) They're so cute.

   (d) I think they're now hiding over there.
4. (a) The Irish Finance Ministers'/Minister's spokesperson was not impressed.

   (b) Jim threw the men's/mens' shoes into the bin.

   (c) The student's/students' noses all turned blue in the cold.

   (d) The baby's/babys' howling could be heard three streets away.
5. (a) Who's going to the party?

   (b) Whose bag is this?
6. (a) Such immature and inconsiderate behaviour fills me with disbelief.

   (b) Unfortunately, we were unaware that the ticket was invalid.

   (c) It was unbelievable that the writing was so illegible.

   (d) Some of the rules were completely irrelevant.
7. (a) How does eating too much chocolate effect/affect your blood sugar?

   (b) We should of/have brought hats and umbrellas with us.

   (c) The principle/principal ingredients of bread are flour, water and yeast.

   (d) Deirdre will not be able to accept/except the new job offer.
8. The button on my sleeve is loose and if I lose that button, I am in serious trouble.
9. The great American writer Mark Twain once said: 'When I was a boy of 14, my father was so ignorant I could hardly stand to have the old man around. But when I got to be 21, I was astonished at how much the old man had learned in seven years.'
10. 'Have you found the advanced philosophy course interesting, my dear?' he asked. His tone indicated that he was a little fearful she might say no. He peered over his half-glasses.

    'Oh, Dr Morgan, how could it be otherwise, when we have the benefit of such an amazingly awesome mind like yours applying itself to the greatest, most profound, issues of the human condition?'

    'Yes, indeed, I'm glad you noticed that,' he intoned.

    'Not to mention that you're such a totally charming gentleman.' Ciara batted her eyes at him, sending a shower of mascara down his eye-catching lurid pink tie.

    'Charming is good... Keep talking,' Morgan mumbled, as he stuffed one of the ridiculously small sandwiches into his mouth.

ACKNOWLEDGEMENTS

Extract from *The Grapes of Wrath* by John Steinbeck. (Copyright 1939, renewed © 1967 by John Steinbeck.) Used by permission of Viking Books, an imprint of Penguin Publishing Group, a division of Penguin Random House LLC.

'Sunday Miscellany: Images of Constance Markievicz' by Ivy Bannister reproduced by kind permission of the author.

'The Road to Wigan Pier' by George Orwell, (Victor Gollancz 1937, Martin Secker & Warburg 1959, Penguin Books 1962, 1989, Penguin Classics 2001). Copyright 1937 by Eric Blair. This edition copyright © the Estate of the late Sonia Brownwell Orwell, 1986. Reproduced by permission of Penguin Books Ltd.

Extract from *India* by Sanjeev Bhaskar, reprinted by permission of HarperCollins Publishers Ltd © (2008) (Sanjeev Bhaskar).

'The Big Debate: Canines or Felines' by Lara Marlowe and Karlin Lililington, The Irish Times, ('Weekend', p. 5, Saturday, February 6th 2016). Reproduced by permission of the authors and The Irish Times.

Extract from *Beatlebone* by Kevin Barry, Canongate, 2015. (Copyright © Kevin Barry 2015) reproduced by kind permission of the author and Canongate.

'Moscow Weekend Break' by Laura Gozzi, Urban Travel Blog (http://www.urbantravelblog.com/guide/moscow/), first published 23rd March 2016, updated September 23rd 2016, reproduced with kind permission of the author and urbantravelblog.com.

'How Groundhog Day Changed My Life' by Paul Hannam, theguardian.com, February 7th 2016. Copyright © Guardian News & Media Ltd 2016. Reproduced with permission of Guardian News & Media Ltd.

Diary entry by Dr Clare O' Leary first published in Ireland on Sunday 23rd May 2004, reproduced courtesy of *Irish Mail on Sunday.*

Extract from *Unreliable Memoirs* by Clive James, Picador, 2008 (First published 1980)

Extract from *The Great Gatsby*, F Scott Fitzgerald, Simon & Schuster, (Scribner 2004)

Extract from *To Kill a Mockingbird*, by Harper Lee, Harper Perennial, imprint of HarperCollins. (Copyright © Harper Lee 1960)

Extract form *Solar* Ian McEwan, Vintage, 2016. First published in Great Britain by Jonathan Cape, 2010. First published by Vintage 2011, reprinted by Vintage 2016 (Copyright © Ian McEwan 2010)

Extract from *In Patagonia* by Bruce Chatwin, Vintage, 2005. First published in Great Britain in 1977 by Jonathan Cape. First published by Vintage in 1998, republished by Vintage in 2005. (Copyright © Bruce Chatwin 1977)